A BASIC GUIDE TO DOG TRAINING AND OBEDIENCE

ABRIDGED EDITION

A BASIC GUIDE TO DOG TRAINING AND OBEDIENCE

BY MARGARET ENGLISH

ABRIDGED EDITION

GROSSET & DUNLAP
PUBLISHERS · NEW YORK

Published simultaneously in Canada
Library of Congress catalog card number: 74-27943
ISBN: 0-448-16329-2
Printed in the United States of America
1982 printing abridged edition

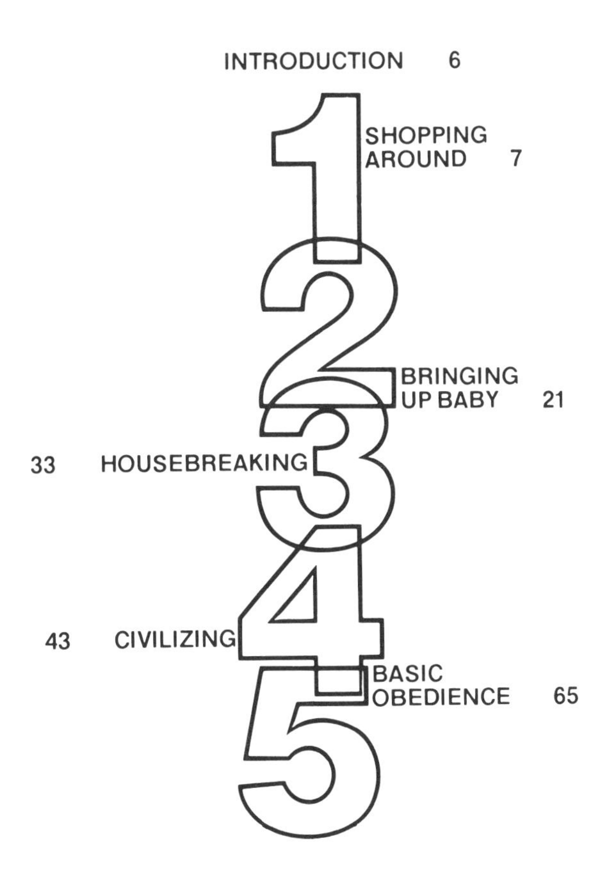

INTRODUCTION

This book is written for everyone who thinks it's fun to have a dog around. Nothing fancy, just a nice dog who'll welcome you home when no one else is speaking to you, laugh at all your worst jokes, and maybe bark at a burglar if the need arises.

Having a dog these days means living pretty close to him. He'll share your home, your car, your sidewalks, and probably your icebox. He'll have to fit into the close, complex society you live in. To do that, he'll have to learn to behave himself. He has to be housebroken, he has to learn not to chew up your furniture, jump up on everyone who comes to the door, or chase cars. He'll need to walk like a gentleman on-lead, ride on the back seat like a chauffeured aristocrat, and socialize with the charm and dignity of an ambassador. Once the first bloom of puppy love has faded, you'll discover that your dog was not born knowing all these things. He was, however, born with a capacity to learn them.

Dogs are uniquely suited to human society. Because your puppy is descended from den dwellers who never fouled their own nests, he has an instinctive respect for household cleanliness, believe it or not. You'll use that instinct to housebreak him.

Your dog's wild ancestors lived and hunted in packs. The survival of the individual depended on the survival of the pack. In turn, the survival of the pack depended on the cooperation of its individual members, who learned and followed a set of strict social rules. Wolf cubs aren't born knowing the bylaws of the pack; they learn them. Your puppy wasn't born knowing how to behave in an apartment house, but he has an instinctive aptitude for absorbing social rules. He learns simply because it's his nature to learn. All you have to do is teach him. I hope that this book will show you how to do it.

Then you'll discover, as I did, that a well-trained dog is more fun to have around than an untrained one.

1 SHOPPING AROUND

If the puppy you bought yesterday has already done something unspeakable to your floor, turn straight to Chapter 2. This chapter is for people who bought the book before the puppy and is written with the hope that it will help you choose just the right dog for yourself.

Perhaps you're wondering whether you should have a dog at all. You have a small apartment in a big city. You go out to work all day. You have allergies, fussy neighbors, small children. None of these drawbacks need prevent you from having a dog if you want one; they only make it a little more complicated.

If your apartment doesn't cramp you, it shouldn't cramp a small dog or even a big lethargic one. Dogs have adapted to living wherever people live. So far, they've gotten along quite comfortably in caves, high-rises, and houseboats; and I'm sure it's only a matter of time before one takes up residence on a space station.

It is not cruel to keep a dog in the city. City pets are generally healthier, cleaner, and less accident-prone than their country cousins. When you live in one room with a dog, you tend to bathe and groom him more often than someone whose pet lives in a doghouse. If your dog is always walked on-lead, he's less likely to be hit by a car or get into fights with other dogs. Finally, if you have to curb him and clean up after him, you stay on top of his digestive problems. For all these reasons the city dog is healthier and safer than one that's allowed to run loose in the country. (The fact that many suburban towns are passing leash and litter laws is helping to extend the benefits of city life to more and more dogs every year.)

Many people who are allergic to dog hair can tolerate certain breeds. Poodles and schnauzers, for example, are often less offensive to people with allergies. Some allergy sufferers can tolerate a small, short-haired dog that can be bathed and groomed frequently without a lot of trouble. In any case, check with your allergist; you may find that, with treatment, you can have a dog if you want one.

If you must leave a dog home alone all day, you do have a problem, but not an insurmountable one. It's not confinement that your dog hates so much as loneliness and boredom. You're going to have to make a special point of devoting some of your nonworking time to his needs, both physical and emotional. If you're not at home to correct his mistakes when he makes them, you'll have to train your dog differently from the person who is. Your emphasis will be on prevention rather than correction. As long as your job permits you to keep a regular feeding and exercise schedule, you and your dog ought to be able to adapt to each other.

Once you've decided to get a dog, your next job is to find one. Stay out of pet shops until you finish this chapter. Your first consideration is yourself, your physical and emotional capabilities, and your life-style.

Even though handling a large dog is more a matter of timing than strength, consider whether or not you have the agility and balance to control a large dog on a leash. Do you have the time and stamina to accompany him on the long walks he'll need to keep fit? An average healthy adult can handle just about any dog, but if your pet is to be walked by a child or an elderly person, stick to the smaller, lightweight breeds.

If you're jumpy or high-strung, don't buy a nervous, high-energy dog; you'll drive each other crazy. If you're afraid of people on the street, resist the temptation to protect yourself with an aggressive dog; your fears may provoke him to the point of viciousness. How authoritarian are you? If you expect instant and perfect obedience at all times, you'll be happiest with one of the more trainable working types like a Border collie or German shepherd who will snap to attention as soon as you call reveille. You'll be miserable with a hound who will stubbornly ignore your commands or a terrier who will tell you just what to do with them.

Be honest now—are you likely to spoil your dog? If so, try to find one that can take a little spoiling without becoming a nuisance. Tyrants, of course, come in all sizes, and even a Chihuahua can dictate your every move if you let him. However, if you're not going to keep your dog off the furniture—and there's no law that says you have to—you'll be happier with one that sheds less than most. If you won't stop him from jumping up on people, get one that can't knock anyone down. If he's going to sleep on your bed, you should know that bulldogs and other short-nosed breeds are notorious snorers, and that dachshunds aren't happy unless they can get under the covers. Dachshund owners consider this one of the breed's finer points, incidentally.

Are you afraid of dogs? A lot of dog owners are, and this is the source of many training problems. A constant fear of being bitten will affect the way you handle your dog. Your wariness could make him shy and snappy. Any rambunctious dog may try growling at you someday just to test your reaction. Are you prepared to let him know that you won't put up with that kind of nonsense? It's very unlikely that your own dog will ever bite you, except in moments of severe stress or panic, but if he discovers that you're afraid he will, he can do a terrific job of bluffing you. This is at the bottom of most dog owners' complaints that begin "He won't . . ." ("He won't get out of my chair. He steals my shoes and won't give them back.") More often than not, "He won't . . ." can be translated into "I'm afraid to make him . . ."

If you're afraid to confront a dog, think about getting a nice box turtle instead.

Now let's consider your family and life-style. Generally speaking, dogs and children are made for each other. However, kids are rough with dogs.

They push them around, dress them up, sit on them, pull their ears, poke their eyes, and step on their tails. And most dogs love it—at least the sturdy ones do. If you have young children, avoid toy breeds such as Chihuahuas or Yorkshire terriers. Stick to a medium-sized breed that can take anything the kids dish out or shrug them off and run away if they get too rough. A tiny dog has no defense but his teeth, and he'll use them if driven to it.

I realize that thousands of large-dog-owning families will disagree with me on this point, but, personally, I would stay away from the giant breeds if I had small children. Even though large dogs are usually better with children than little dogs, what might be a simple nip from a cocker spaniel will be a major wound if inflicted by a Great Dane. Perhaps I'm being overcautious, but it seems to me that if you have a choice, you might as well make a safe one.

Even if you have a small apartment, there's no real reason why you can't have a large dog. Lots of people do. They manage by getting their dogs out to a park or suburb and giving them a good hard run several times a week. If you can't take the time or can't train your dog well enough to keep control of him when he's running off-lead, stick to a short-legged breed that will get all the exercise he needs on a trip to the newsstand and back. Don't, however, get a basset hound or a dachshund if you live in a fourth-floor walk-up. They don't climb stairs well.

All this adds up to taking a good look at yourself and your environment, and deciding what kind of dog will best adjust. No matter where you live, chances are there is a dog that can adapt himself to your home. It's your job to find him.

Which sex should you get? Most people choose whichever sex the dog they like happens to be and live happily ever after. It's not a steadfast rule that males roam more than females. Of course, if a neighborhood bitch is in season, your male is likely to want to camp on her doorstep for the duration. On the other hand, your female beagle is just as likely to take off for a weekend of rabbit hunting—or garbage collecting—whenever the mood strikes her. Moreover, in these days of leash laws and dog wardens, your dog may not have the freedom to roam anyway.

Males do tend to be more aggressive than females, and you will have to worry more about dog fights if you get a male. On the other hand, you won't have to worry about his becoming an unwed mother. Both worries can be reduced or eliminated by neutering.

In general, the temperamental differences between dogs are derived from their individual natures and upbringing rather than from their sex. So, unless you plan to breed dogs, sex should not be a major factor in your choice of a pet for a one-dog family. I should mention, however, that if you plan to keep your dog paper-trained through adulthood, you'll probably do better with a female. A small male can be trained to lift his leg against an overturned flowerpot placed on newspapers, but even if he has terrific aim, it's one more thing to clean up.

Unless you have a specific reason for buying an adult dog—for example, a show prospect or a trained hunting dog—look for a six- to eight-week-old puppy. At that age, he's just left his mother and is in the market for a substitute; you'll be the one he's looking for. An older dog will probably have fastened his affection onto someone else, and you'll have a tough time winning him over. On the other hand, he may have lacked human attention—or received the wrong kind—as a puppy and may never become properly socialized to human beings. Canine behaviorists have discovered that puppies kept caged and isolated from humans from the age of five to eight weeks rarely recover fully from the experience; they remain unresponsive to human affection, shy, frightened, and suspicious for the rest of their lives. Even though you might make a few mistakes raising your puppy, at least they'll be *your* mistakes. And your dog will probably love you in spite of them.

Which breed should you get? Whatever suits you. You're the best judge of the physical characteristics that best suit your home, family, and aesthetic taste. However, you need to consider more than size and style; many breeds have peculiar characteristics that you should know about before you choose. Short-nosed dogs are prone to respiratory problems. Floppy-eared breeds are susceptible to ear trouble, dachshunds to slipped discs. Be wary of hip dysplasia, a hereditary degeneration of the hip joints, in the large breeds, *especially* German shepherds.

Before you make your final decision on any breed, call a veterinarian and find out what health problems you may have to cope with. Extra vet bills for a delicate breed may well influence your decision.

There are more myths about breed differences in temperament and personality than I care to count: poodles are supposed to be geniuses, Dobermans vicious, retrievers gentle, etc., etc. Actually, there are enough stupid, sweet, and belligerent exceptions to make the myths about as believable as *Sir Gawain and the Green Knight*. There are, however, real differences among breed groups, and you'll need to consider them in your choice. Over the centuries, different types of dogs were bred to perform different tasks. To those ends, certain instinctive traits were selectively emphasized or eliminated. Hounds, for instance, were used to pursue, capture, or corner game; those with the most pronounced hunting instincts were bred to one another, and this trait was inherited by their offspring. Other qualities were ignored and bred out. In the case of hounds, these qualities included a high degree of trainability. Hounds lived in kennels, hunted in packs, and didn't need to know a lot of fancy commands and signals. They did their job well, and they did it by instinct. Anyone who's ever tried to call a beagle off a squirrel trail understands the problem.

This doesn't mean that hounds make poor pets. On the contrary, there is nothing like an Afghan for elegance or a basset for laughs. They can certainly be civilized for family living, housebroken, leash trained, and taught not to chew up the furniture. They have even, with patient, skilled handling, won advanced obedience titles. But it ain't easy. Incidentally, pack hounds, such as beagles and foxhounds, are generally considered to be more tolerant of other dogs than most. There are exceptions, of course. One of them is my mother's beagle, Lucy, named after the "Peanuts" character whose truculent temperament she shares.

The terrier is another dog whose instincts make him difficult to train. Terriers are cute, funny, sprightly, sassy, and almost frustrating enough to make you stop loving them. Back in the Merrie Olde Days, when the foxhounds had chased the fox into his hole and stood around baying like blazes and congratulating themselves, the huntsman would ride up and pull a fox terrier out of his saddlebag. And guess who'd go down into the hole and nail that fox? Anything that man is afraid to reach in after with his bare hand, he's bred a terrier to kill for him—rats, foxes, weasels, you name it. That's the kind of nerve you're up against when you come home and tell your Scotty to go fetch your slippers and he tells you to go fetch yourself.

I'm not suggesting that terriers make miserable pets. Like all dogs, they're naturally inclined to love people—thank goodness. They are charming, debonaire, loyal, and lovable. And absolutely fearless. You won't get anywhere with a terrier by trying to browbeat him or scare him. Your best tactic is to be even more stubborn than he is; correct him when he's bad, praise him when he's good, and hang in there. Your toughest problem with terriers is their extreme intolerance of other dogs. They are born fighters, and, unlike other breeds, won't give up a losing battle. If you must have more than one, your best bet is to limit yourself to two of opposite sexes (males and females will squabble but rarely get into a serious fight) or switch to another breed and let the terrier boss the other one around. When you're away from home, keep your terrier on a leash or be ready to bail him out of trouble at a moment's notice.

Despite all this, terriers are very popular pets, much prized for their style and gutsiness. None of the above is intended to discourage you from owning one but simply to let you know that you're not getting a Shetland sheepdog.

The Sheltie is a working dog like the collie, German shepherd, boxer, Great Dane, malamute, and corgi. They are all bred for work—herding cattle or sheep, guarding property, even pulling carts and sleds. As a rule, they are the most trainable of dogs, and, along with poodles and retrievers, tend to dominate dog show obedience classes. They have been bred for their physical adaptability to their tasks and their willingness to take direction from humans. Ironically, the German shepherd and the Doberman pinscher, two breeds considered vicious by myth-spreaders, fall into this category. Their false reputation probably stems from their historic use as guard dogs. Yet a good guard dog need not be vicious and, in fact, shouldn't be. Anyone can make a dog vicious. I suspect that people who want nasty dogs buy breeds with nasty reputations and then encourage them to be so. Actually, most of the Dobermans I've met are cloyingly friendly, and I'm sure they don't pick German shepherds to guide the blind because of their viciousness.

The working breeds tend to be rugged outdoorsy types. Although it's difficult to imagine Queen Elizabeth's corgis rounding up cattle, that's what they were bred for. This will sound peculiar, but a working dog needs to be kept busy. If you don't have any cattle or sheep, think of something else for him to do. By and large, the working breeds will take as much training as you can give them. Any puppy can be developed into a reasonably well-behaved house pet, but the working dogs are bred for advanced training and thrive on it.

There are, of course, variations within the working group. Huskies and malamutes, considered by canine experts to be the closest domestic relation to the wolf, need a firm hand and seem, to me, anyway, to be among the least trainable of the working breeds. At the other end of the spectrum are Shetland sheepdogs. The Sheltie, or miniature collie, comes from the Shetland Islands, which produced dwarf cattle, dwarf sheep, and dwarf herding dogs. He is considered to be one of the finest working dogs in the world. Shelties are bright, willing, sensitive little dogs that, with gentle handling, can learn just about anything. Rumor has it that they can take telephone messages.

While we're on the subject, please don't confuse trainability with intelligence. Canine IQ studies have indicated that all breeds are about equally intelligent. That is, they're all equally adept at getting out of mazes, putting square pegs in square holes, answering multiple-choice questions, and passing whatever laboratory tests are devised for making such judgments—none of which has anything to do with how quickly they can learn to hold it until morning.

The sporting breeds are bred to find, flush, point at, or retrieve birds. In general, they are more trainable than hounds but have a stronger hunting instinct, and are, therefore, more distractable than the working breeds. Bird dogs are valued for their light mouths, and a good retriever can carry a raw egg without breaking it or a live bird without ruffling its feathers. This doesn't mean they won't bite. All dogs bite when they feel they have to.

The sporting breeds, like the working dogs, need exercise and work. If you plan to keep one in an apartment, be prepared to get him out and running as often as possible.

A retriever owner once told me, "Hit a Chesapeake with a baseball bat, a Labrador with a ruler, and a golden with a wet Kleenex." I'm not sure you have to hit *any* dog, but I pass the remark along simply as a retriever fancier's impression of the sensitivity of the three breeds. In my experience, goldens do seem more eager to please and Chesapeakes more stubborn, but don't blame me if you get a bull-headed goldie.

Of all the breeds, only the toys were bred strictly as house pets. It was their job to sit on laps, dish out affection, and soak up all the goodies that indulgent humans would shower on them. Toy poodles, Pomeranians, Pekinese, Chihuahuas, and pugs all fall into this pampered group, which is not as frivolous as it might seem. A great many elderly, lonely people are kept alive, active, and interested by the only dogs they could possibly keep—toys. I might be ready for one myself in a few years.

The toys are delicate creatures. They need tender care, coats in the winter, shade in the summer. They were born to be spoiled. They like cozy beds (especially yours), gourmet food, toys, clothes, jewelry, the works. So lay it on—that's what you got him for.

A poor choice for families with young children, the toys are naturally skittish. If you wonder why, lie on the floor and look up at someone standing over you. Anyone who trains a toy must be very gentle but must also resist the temptation to baby him. Fortunately, a dog that weighs four pounds doesn't need much training.

The toys' obvious advantage is convenience. You can pop a Pomeranian in a shopping bag and take him on the bus. You can keep him paper-trained for life so you never have to take him for subzero midnight walks. Toys make excellent pets for older people and apartment dwellers. Most of us buy dogs for companionship, and toys have plenty to give. Even though my own taste runs to big dogs, I'd take a Pekinese over a gerbil any day.

It's difficult to characterize the nonsporting breeds. Although several were once hunting or working dogs, the only thing they all have in common is that they no longer quite fit into any of the other groups. Among the most popular are the Dalmatian, the Lhasa apso, and the most popular dog in the United States, the poodle. Poodles come in three sizes: toy (under ten inches at the shoulder), miniature (ten to fifteen inches), and standard (fifteen inches and over). The standards, incidentally, are getting bigger all the time. Show-quality males are now running a good twenty-five inches or so.

Poodles deserve their popularity; they are clever, energetic, responsive, highly trainable, and born show-offs. They are also born goof-offs. A poodle can perform spectacularly in the obedience ring one day and behave as if he'd never left the whelping box the next. He considers this part of his charm.

The poodle's coat and ears need plenty of attention. Because of his floppy ears and thick hair, his ear passages can easily become clogged with wax and dirt; hence, they need regular cleaning. His coat will grow practically forever if you don't clip it. Hair that is shed stays in the coat and forms mats if not regularly brushed out. Don't let this discourage you, however. With a comb, a brush, a good pair of clippers, and a little confidence, anyone can keep a poodle neatly groomed.

Because show-quality miniature poodles are bred very close to the maximum height of fifteen inches, some grow over the limit and become small standards. They're too small for the show ring but make nice medium-sized house pets. So, if you're thinking about a small standard poodle, check with the mini breeders. You might even get a bargain.

Finally, there's the good old American mongrel, or mixed-breed. He can be healthy, wise, and a model of poise and stability; he can also be genetically unsound, retarded, and a maniac. It's hard to tell until you get him home, and that's the problem. When you breed two beagles, you know in advance that your puppies will look and act like beagles. A mongrel puppy can inherit characteristics from one or all of dozens of ancestors; he may have the conformation of three different breeds and the temperament of a fourth.

One of the mongrel's advantages is that he'll fit almost anybody's budget, since he's usually either given away or placed by an animal shelter for a minimal fee. You can't touch a purebred dog for much under a hundred dollars anymore.

The right breed for you might be one you've never seen or one you didn't even know existed. In that case, go where the dogs are—to a dog show. Let's say you love the look of some of the shaggy terriers but can't stand the terrier temperament. There's your dog in ring #4, a Tibetan terrier. Despite his name and looks, he's a member of the nonsporting group and has a far more peace-loving personality than most terriers. Maybe you're dreaming of an Old English sheepdog, but you haven't got the space or the energy to cope with anything that big. Your dog could be over in the miscellaneous ring—a bearded collie. He looks like a little sheepdog with a tail.

After you've decided on the breed or nonbreed you want, the next step is to find your particular dog. Unless you have good reason to do otherwise, I would advise buying a purebred dog from a breeder. He knows his breed, understands its special needs, and is best equipped to tell you how to care for it. He knows his dogs' pedigrees and can tell you what inherited characteristics he expects your puppy to have. Also, he'll probably have your dog's mother on the premises. Take a good look at her; she's 50 percent of what your puppy will be. Introduce yourself to her. Is she friendly and relaxed with you or shy and nervy? She has been the major influence on your puppy for the last six to eight weeks, and his basic attitude toward people will probably be much like hers. Get to know her.

To find a breeder in your area, write to the American Kennel Club, 51 Madison Avenue, New York, New York 10010. Tell them what breed you're interested in, and they'll send you a list of breeders.

Don't forget to check the classified section of your local newspaper for home-raised puppies. For a family dog, a home-bred puppy is often the best bet. This is particularly true of mongrels but goes for purebred dogs as well. A puppy who has spent the first weeks of his life in a home like yours is already well on his way to adapting himself to your life-style; he'll have no trouble getting used to your kids if he's had a couple of them playing with him for the past month or so. Here, too, you'll have a chance to meet the puppy's mother and his owner. Watch how the owner handles the puppies. Is he rough or gentle? How do they respond? A six-week-old puppy who has been handled properly will be outgoing, playful, and deliriously affectionate. If he's not, there's something wrong.

If you're looking for a mongrel, by all means try to get him from a family. In this way you'll be able to find out something about his background and have a chance to meet his mother. The owners might even know who the father is, but don't count on it. In any case, it stands to reason that folks who take the trouble to find homes for their puppies and assume the expense of placing an ad in the paper will have raised them more carefully than people who dump puppies in an animal shelter.

Animal shelters, bless them, serve a crucial function in the dog world and deserve far more support than they get. Unfortunately, you face a number of problems when you adopt a puppy from one: you have little chance of getting any reliable information about your puppy's background; you'll be adopting a mongrel puppy without seeing his mother or having a chance to inspect the home he came from; you can only guess at what he'll be like when he grows up. The few assumptions you can safely make aren't very encouraging: the people who left him there didn't care enough to find him a good home on their own; no one wanted him, or he wouldn't be there; he's been living in a cage with minimal attention during the very stage of his development when he most needs affectionate human contact.

I hate to paint such a grim picture, but these are the sad facts of the animal shelter business. And I certainly don't mean to denigrate the sincere efforts of the people and organizations who run them. They are generally humane, caring animal lovers who do the best they can at an underfinanced, discouraging job.

You can protect yourself to some extent. Look for a young puppy who has been in the shelter for a very short time. The sooner he gets out and starts socializing, the better pet he'll be. Many wonderful dogs have been adopted from animal shelters, and I don't mean to discourage you from getting yours there. Most dogs are remarkably sturdy creatures and, given proper care, can recover from almost anything. If you make a careful choice and give your puppy plenty of loving attention when you get him home, you stand an excellent chance of adopting a fine companion.

Finally, a word about pet shops. Of all the places to get a puppy, a pet shop should be your *last* choice. I realize that many people have bought fine dogs from shops, but a good many others have been stung. Too many pet shops, particularly the chain stores that specialize in purebred dogs, acquire their puppies from mass-production breeders whose sole aim is to produce as many animals as possible for the retail market. Virtually no attention is paid to breed standard or temperament, and no attempt is made to eliminate genetic weaknesses.

The American Dog Owners Association has documented any number of outright frauds perpetrated by pet shops, chain stores, and department stores. They include the sale, for a good price, I'm sure, of a completely blind puppy, the sale of puppies with distemper, fraudulent registration, and the sale of a purported purebred St. Bernard that was declared by three licensed judges to be of mixed ancestry.

Even in relatively honest shops, most puppies are victims of transport stress. You'll read more about this in the chapter on traveling with your dog. For the moment, remember that that pet-shop puppy has been taken from his mother at the minimum age allowable by law—an extremely vulnerable age—crammed into a crate that may or may not have been suitably constructed for the shipment of live animals, and transported across the country like any other piece of freight. Not long ago, a New York TV station turned up a batch of puppies stranded at an airport during a strike. They were destined for a pet shop and packed in what appeared to be a lettuce crate. The terror, discomfort, and probably unhealthy conditions a pet-shop puppy has suffered during his trip have left him traumatized, exhausted, and more susceptible to disease than a normal puppy. And when he reaches his destination, he's put on display to await rescue. The best way to rescue pet-shop puppies is not to buy them but to put the people who deal in them out of business.

Under ideal conditions, a pet shop would buy puppies from local breeders, keep litters together, keep complete, accurate pedigree records, maintain the strictest sanitary conditions, and see to it that all the puppies had regular play periods every day with affectionate, gentle humans. If you ever find a pet shop that meets these standards—and there may well be one somewhere—feel free to buy a puppy. It will deserve your business. However, the chances of finding a shop like this are pretty slim. With a little extra effort and no extra cost, you can buy your puppy direct from his breeder and stand a better chance of getting the kind of dog you want.

Okay. The great day has arrived. You've decided on the breed you want and have found a litter of puppies from which to make your choice. Now you really have to get tough, because there is no such thing as an unadorable puppy. At this point, most people just relax and let the magic take effect. You sit down and look at the litter, and pretty soon your dog makes himself known. You don't know how it happened, but somehow the two of you have found each other. Don't knock it. People get married in much the same way, and, despite the divorce statistics, it usually works.

Do try to keep your wits about you, though. It's awfully easy to fall in love with the wrong puppy. Every litter has a right one and a wrong one. At six weeks, each puppy will already have acquired much of his basic temperament and personality. You'll be able to modify it, but you won't be able to change it. The shy one, who sits in the corner impressing you with his serene dignity, will never become gregarious. With gentle handling, he may, as he gains maturity and confidence, become reserved rather than fearful; but he'll never be the life of the party. The bully of the litter, the one who muscles all the others aside to get to you first, will want to go right on being a bully at home. If you're not prepared to really assert yourself with him, leave him for someone who is.

By the time puppies are old enough to be sold, they have begun to sort themselves into a recognizable social order within the litter. One will boss all the others around, helping himself to the lion's share of all the food, toys, and attention available. Another will back away from any conflict, giving way to every other puppy in the litter. Those in between will have figured out roughly where they stand, bullying some and giving way to others. Watching the puppies play and compete with each other will help you decide which one you'll best be able to live with. Incidentally, if you're looking for a female to breed someday, try to avoid a really bossy one; she may prove difficult to breed, male dogs being dreadful chauvinists. In general, unless you have a definite reason for wanting a highly aggressive or submissive dog, look for a puppy that falls somewhere in the middle of the litter's pecking order.

Your next job is to determine how well your puppy relates to you. Of course he'll like you; you wouldn't want one that didn't. Pick a puppy up and carry him away from the litter. Does he cry and try to squirm away, or does he settle down and snuggle in your arms? Put him down, roll him over on his back, and hold him still. Does he struggle and nip, or does he relax and accept your dominance? At this age, puppies should respond to gentle, affectionate handling in a relaxed, trusting, submissive way.

Dr. Michael Fox, canine psychologist and author of *Understanding Your Dog,* suggests several tests whereby you can judge the socialization and trainability of a young puppy. You might, with the breeder's permission, try a couple of them.

First, take the puppy away from the litter and place him on a low box or step. How quickly does he jump down? Puppies are supposed to be adventurous. One that absolutely refuses to jump may be too timid. How quickly does a puppy who's afraid at first jump by himself after you've helped him a couple of times? Although Fox doesn't say so, this seems to me to be an excellent indication of the qualities to look for in a pet. Even though a puppy may be frightened at first, he should trust you enough to accept your help and direction. This could be the start of a great relationship.

Fox also suggests that you get a rag or towel and play tug-of-war with each puppy. Does he pull vigorously or give up easily? If you want a very submissive puppy, pick one who lets you win. Most of them will hang on, however, so try the next test. Let go of the towel. A normal puppy will run away with it, shaking and mouthing it. This is the normal prey-killing instinct at work. Now, see whether he surrenders the towel readily when you try to get it back or runs farther away with it. If he won't give it up, he may be too possessive. He may grow into a dog who will snap when you approach his food dish or bed. Look for a puppy who either gives up the towel or brings it back to you inviting more play. Most dogs learn pretty quickly that it takes two to play tug-of-war.

Animal behaviorists have more tests with which they can evaluate a puppy's temperament, but most of them are too elaborate and clinical for the average dog owner to worry about. Furthermore, like computer dating services, they tend to take the romance out of it all. You should fall in love with your puppy. Just try to fall in love with one whose basic temperament suits your own. If you're a tough, no-nonsense type and can assume a dominant role with a rambunctious, aggressive dog, pick the bruiser of the litter, the one who launches himself nose first off the box and who'll tug on a towel all day. You'll be able to handle him, and he'll be tough enough to take it without being terrorized. If you're easygoing, permissive, and inclined to spoil your dog a little, pick a more submissive puppy who'll respond to gentle corrections and won't take advantage of your good nature.

Finally, be sure you get a healthy puppy. Don't let anyone tell you that he just has a little cold that will clear up in a few days, or that the reason he seems listless is because he was playing hard before you arrived. Cold symptoms could be a sign of distemper. General listlessness could indicate that the puppy is sick or infested with parasites. Even if he seems healthy to you, have his temperature taken. It should be about 101.5° F. Get a certified record of his inoculations, and find out whether or not he's been wormed and for which type of worm.

Once you've made your choice, try to arrange to take him on a trial basis and have him examined by a vet before you take permanent possession. Better to be safe than saddled with a sick puppy and extra vet bills.

If you buy a purebred dog, the breeder or dealer should provide you with a copy of his pedigree (family tree) and an application form for registering him with the American Kennel Club. This application form will show his parents' registration numbers, his date of birth, and his litter number. This is *not* a registration certificate, only an application for one. After you have filled it out and mailed it in with a four-dollar fee, the AKC will send you a certificate of your dog's registration. If you plan to show your dog, he must be registered. If you plan to breed him or her, the dog must be registered so you can sell your puppies for what they're worth.

If for any reason the breeder does not have your puppy's application form or other transfer papers available when you pick him up, insist that he give you a signed bill of sale indicating your puppy's breed, sex, color, markings, date of birth, the names and numbers of his parents, and his litter number. All this information must conform to the data on your application form when the dealer finally delivers it. Your bill of sale should also provide for refund of the purchase price and return of the dog if the application form is not delivered.

Thousands of puppies are advertised as "AKC registered" even though they may not be registered and possibly cannot be. This might be because the seller mistakenly believes that an application form or a pedigree certificate constitutes actual registration. It might also be that he's trying to gyp you. Be suspicious. Don't take the puppy without a completed application form or a detailed bill of sale. If you're paying purebred prices, you're entitled to purebred proof.

2 BRINGING UP BABY

Now that you've chosen the best puppy in the world, you'll have to think of a name for him. You can name your dog after your favorite literary character, movie star, or Watergate co-conspirator. Some people make up terribly clever, sophisticated names for their dogs, and practically everybody else picks Brandy, Missy, or Duke. Be as creative as you like, but give your dog a name he can understand and that will get his attention when you say it; i.e., keep it short and snappy. Two syllables are about all he can take. If you have more than one dog, try to give them names with different vowel sounds—like Sam, Pete, Millie, Spot, and Lucy. That way, they'll know which one you're calling. Avoid names that sound too much like "come," "heel," "sit," "down," and "stay." You'll have enough trouble teaching him all those things without him thinking you're just saying his name twice. You probably shouldn't use a name that sounds like that of someone in your family, although I'm not sure this is really important. My sister Susie once had a roommate who had a dog named Susie, and the dog always knew which one you were talking about.

Dogs have excellent hearing, but they're not verbal. After a while, they get used to hearing and ignoring a constant stream of nonsense from you. A complicated name can get lost in a cascade of meaningless sounds. You'll find it easier to get your dog's attention if you give him a name he can pick out easily.

When you go to get your puppy, take along a blanket if the weather is cool, and a roll of paper towels. Puppies are notoriously prone to car sickness. His breeder will probably have sense enough not to feed him before you arrive, but you can't always count on good sense in this world. Take someone with you who can drive or hold the puppy on the way home. This will probably be his first automobile ride, and he should find it either very scary or utterly thrilling. In either case, someone should be there to reassure him or hold him still.

Have newspapers ready and waiting on the kitchen floor when you get home. Depending on how long a trip your puppy has had, your foresight should be promptly rewarded. Once he's relieved himself, you can let him explore the rest of the house and introduce himself to the rest of the family. Don't overwhelm him at first. He's bound to be tired and a little frightened. Give him enough affection to show that he's with friends, but put off vigorous romping until he's had a good rest.

If you have children, insist that they take it easy for the first few days. They'll have plenty of time next week to play Kung Fu with the puppy. The same goes for you. Don't have a cocktail party for him on the first night home. Give him time to get used to his new surroundings in peace and quiet, and let him figure out whom he belongs to before you introduce him to the rest of the neighborhood.

After your puppy has inspected the premises, he'll probably be ready for a snack, another trip to the newspapers, and a nap. Decide right now where he's going to sleep. And be firm. If he has to sleep anywhere but on your bed or someone else's, he'll scream for his mother, the Humane Society, and a writ of habeas corpus all in one breath. All puppies think they'll die if they don't sleep with somebody, and they all cry the first time they're left alone. Unless you're an awfully good sport about your bedroom carpet, let him scream. He'll get over it. Making your puppy sleep in the kitchen (or some other durable room) until he's grown up will not warp his personality or ruin your relationship with him. No matter what he says, he won't hate you for it. Furthermore, when he's civilized enough to spend the night in your room without destroying it, he won't turn down your invitation.

So, find a draft-free corner of your kitchen for the puppy's bed. It doesn't have to be a fancy wicker job from the pet store. In fact, it shouldn't be until he's old enough to leave it in one piece. For the time being, a folded, preferably washable blanket will do quite nicely. Don't worry about him not realizing that that's his bed; dogs seem to think that anything you leave on the floor—newspapers, towels, clothing—is there for them to lie on. If possible, put his bed under the table. Dogs are descended from den dwellers and feel more secure with something over their heads at night. If you haven't got a table, put his blanket in a corner or against a wall.

If you plan to follow the working person's guide to housebreaking—and it's the best method even if you only clip coupons for a living—you'll need a sturdy wire crate. Good ones are fairly expensive, but they're worth it. You'll need one big enough for your puppy to stand up and turn around in even after he's full grown. Put the crate in a warm corner (with a blanket over the top if it's cold, but don't smother him). Put the puppy's blanket in it. Add a few toys, dog biscuits, and finally the puppy. Don't shut the gate. For the next six weeks or so, the crate will serve only as his bed. He should be able to go in and out of it freely.

Now, line the kitchen floor with papers, shut the door (or mesh baby gate if you have a doorless kitchen), go to bed, and eat your heart out. If you can get the covers over your head before he starts yelling, you've made good time. You might get up a couple of times and say a few soothing words to the little monster or call reassuringly from your bedroom just to let him know he hasn't been abandoned. This probably won't stop him from crying, but it might make you feel a little better. Whatever you do, don't get nasty, and don't take pity on him. The first night is the hardest.

Incidentally, if you have a very small breed, you can put his bed in the corner of the baby's playpen (one he can't get out of) and line the rest of it with newspapers. This will give you a smaller area to clean up and still leave the puppy enough room to relieve himself away from his bed.

You can't get really serious about housebreaking at this stage of the game; your puppy simply won't have enough control of himself until he's at least three months old. This doesn't mean, however, that you can't start off on the right foot. Dogs are naturally clean animals, although their standards may not be quite up to yours. A dog will not soil his own sleeping quarters if he can possibly help it. Even at six weeks, a puppy has already learned to crawl out of the nest when nature calls. This is an instinctive act, although he may have had a little help from his mother who was undoubtedly sick of cleaning up after him. Be glad you don't have her problems. So, when you housebreak a dog, gradually enlarge his concept of the nest to include your house or apartment, hall, elevator, lobby, and sidewalk.

But all this comes later. Until he's old enough to be housebroken, you are responsible for your puppy's personal hygiene. He's likely to urinate as often as twelve times a day (or more—you won't believe it until you see it) and have up to four daily bowel movements. All will be performed with a minimum of warning. People who tell you to catch him when he squats have forgotten how fast it all happens. You can, however, count on the following: he is just about guaranteed to relieve himself right after eating, sleeping, and playing. So be sure to get him onto his newspapers then. If it has occurred to you that puppies do little else but eat, sleep, and play and that you're going to be pretty busy, you're learning fast.

The answer is to confine him to a well-papered area at those times when you expect him to perform and keep a sharp eye on him even when you don't. Puppies are full of surprises, and it's always the same surprise. If you should happen to catch him about to commit an unspeakable act on your living room rug, scoop him up fast and hustle him onto the papers. This may well leave a trail all the way to the kitchen, and you may well wish you hadn't bothered. But this is the only way you'll ever get the idea across. At this age, your puppy is still too young to be punished for his mistakes, so hold your temper and keep him under supervision.

He's never too young to be praised for doing something right, however. Praise him lavishly whenever you see him performing on the papers. This will not only help the puppy get the idea, but it will also be good practice for the day when you have to stand out on the street in front of a dozen strangers waxing lyrical over a pile of you-know-what in the gutter.

As far as dirty newspapers are concerned, no one should have to tell you to replace them as soon as they're soiled. Even if you have a very high tolerance for puppy droppings, you should know that there are dogs in this world who eat such things.

Some trainers suggest that you leave one sheet of paper with a little urine on it down with the fresh ones. This, they say, will inspire the puppy to return to the spot he visited before. I've never noticed any advantage to this. By the time your puppy is old enough to figure out what the newspapers are for, he's smart enough to know a newspaper when he sees one—with or without leftover urine. Make your own decision. It's your kitchen.

Since your dog is bound to have a few accidents, you might as well learn how to get urine out of a rug. After years of trial and error, I can promise you that the following is the best method: Don't start scrubbing right away, you'll only rub it in. Blot up as much as you can with toilet tissue and flush it away. Keep doing this until a fresh tissue comes away dry. Then pour on some club soda to neutralize the acid. Scrub it in with a brush or sponge and let it dry. In a few hours, you'll never know it happened. Incidentally, there is an excellent product called Dogtek that serves the same function as club soda (although it doesn't taste as good with Scotch).

Sometime during the first week, take your puppy to the vet for an examination. Take a stool sample with you; about half a teaspoonful should be enough. Also take whatever inoculation records the breeder or dealer gave you when he sold you the puppy. The vet will give him any additional shots he might need to protect him from distemper, leptospirosis, and canine hepatitis. He'll also tell you when to bring him back for boosters and rabies shots. Don't neglect these shots. Most states require annual rabies vaccinations. Distemper, leptospirosis, or hepatitis may not kill your dog if he's lucky, but they're a lot easier and cheaper to prevent than cure.

The person you bought your puppy from has probably given you complete instructions on what and how often to feed him. He'll most likely be getting at least three meals a day and should be eating prepared dog food. The dry foods such as Wayne, Gaines Meal, or Purina Dog Chow are excellent and far and away the most economical. The premoistened foods such as Prime and Top Choice are good and handy—great for traveling—but they're pretty expensive if you have to feed more than two packages a day. I use canned meat strictly as a supplement to dry food. I know that most manufacturers claim the canned foods provide a complete diet, but if you check the labels, you'll find that they usually contain less of everything, even protein, than the better dry foods.

Some dogs get incredibly exotic menus, probably because their owners enjoy telling their friends what exotic tastes their dogs have. "Foofie won't touch anything but prime ribs and buttered baby peas." Foofie's exotic life will be somewhat shorter as a result. I am a firm believer in dog food—plain dog food. The major companies have put a lot of time and research into developing a balanced, nutritious product, and I advise taking advantage of it. You can add table scraps, canned meat, cottage cheese, anything you like, but dog food should be your dog's staple and should account for at least three-quarters of every meal.

Although the major brands of dog food are supposed to contain all the vitamins your dog needs, it can't hurt to give him a few extra, especially if he's still growing. Canine vitamin tablets (Pervinal and Theralin are the most popular) are available in most pet shops and from food suppliers. Just about any dog will eat them in his food or as a treat. Also, ask your vet about a calcium supplement. If you've got a growing Great Dane or some other large breed on your hands, he's going to need all the bone builders he can get.

If you have a very, very active dog or puppy, he may not get enough fat from plain dog food. Most prepared foods are less than 8 percent fat. If you have a hard-working dog or an active puppy, he may need as much as 10 to 20 percent. You can judge your dog's fat requirement from the condition of his coat. If it's shiny and healthy looking, he's probably getting along just fine; if it becomes dry and dull, and his skin looks scaly, add pan drippings, vegetable oil, or even a little lard to his dinners. If his stools become loose, give him less fat.

If you're one of those lucky people whose dog likes dry food right out of the box and doesn't overeat, you can put him on a self-feeding program. Just leave a bowl of dry food down all the time and let him eat whenever he feels like it. Remember to keep water available all the time as well. Don't start this until he's thoroughly housebroken, however, because meal scheduling is half the battle in housebreaking.

Although your puppy is still too young for serious training, it's never too soon to begin establishing the habits and patterns you'll build on when you do get serious. First of all, use the puppy's name frequently when you talk to him and play with him. Whenever you call him to you, use the same words you'll use when you start to train him: "Puppy (or whatever his name is), come!" Sound enthusiastic when you call him. Get down on the floor, pat your knee, offer him a toy or a biscuit—anything that will attract his attention and get him to come toward you. If he doesn't move, pretend to run away and let him catch you. When he gets to you, praise him in warm, loving tones: "Goooood Puppy. Gooood Boy/Girl." Dogs love those "ooooo" sounds, so drag them out. Pat him, play with him, rub his tummy. Make him feel good all over.

Don't get into the habit of just going to get him whenever you want him. It might seem easier than calling and praising, but that's not how to teach him to come when he's called. On the other hand, never ever call a puppy to you to be punished. That's the best way in the world to teach him to run away when you call. The whole idea is to make him realize that there's something good in it for him whenever he hears "Puppy, come!"

Even if a dog doesn't understand what you're saying, he will respond to your tone of voice. Dogs have very little taste for subtlety. Gush and coo when you praise him; if he doesn't wag his tail when he hears "Goood Boy!" you're not laying it on thick enough. Snarl and snap when you scold. Be melodramatic. Some of the best trainers I've seen sound like the worst kind of nursery school teacher, but it works.

If you live in a city, I think you should avoid taking your puppy out on the street or to a park until he's three months old. City streets are full of parasites and dangerous objects that shouldn't be swallowed by curious puppies. This may seem overcautious, but I can only tell you that my own dog has had to be treated for hookworms and whipworms several times since coming to live in New York, and any vet will tell you that these worms and their treatment are hard on young puppies. Certainly, no puppy should be taken out until he's fully inoculated against distemper, hepatitis, and leptospirosis. If he's had his shots, you can use your own judgment or follow your vet's advice. However, if he were my dog, I'd keep him off the street.

Needless to say, if you have a nice, clean, fenced-in suburban yard, there's no reason why your puppy can't go out to play on warm days. Just keep an eye on him, and bring him in when he gets tired.

Even though you may not be taking your puppy outdoors yet, you can start leash training him at about ten weeks. Buy him a very lightweight buckled collar; a cat collar might be right for a small breed. Don't buy a big expensive one for him to grow into; get a cheap one that you can throw away when he grows out of it. The collar may bother him at first, and he might try to shake or scratch it off. However, if you put it on him just before mealtime, he'll have forgotten all about it by the time he's finished eating. In any case, he should get used to it in a few hours. Don't try to put a lead on him until he's completely accustomed to his collar.

Before you use a real lead, get a piece of light clothesline or venetian blind cord about one and one-half times the length of your puppy's body. Tie one end to his collar, and let him drag it around with him for a while. At first he'll get tangled up, step on the cord, trip himself, and exhibit a general air of befuddlement. Don't laugh at him, and don't leap to the rescue. Let him figure it out. As soon as he learns to get around without tripping, you can exchange the clothesline for a training lead.

The lead should be four to six feet long (the smaller the dog, the longer the lead). Get the lightest one you can find, either braided nylon or cotton webbing. No chains, please. It should have a light clasp that won't bang against the puppy when he moves. Remember, the less weight you have hanging on his neck, the less disturbing all this will be for him.

After you've snapped the lead on the puppy's collar, stand still and talk to him. When he gets bored with your idle chitchat, he'll probably start to move away. Move with him. Keep the lead slack, and let him walk you. If he gets tangled up, explain gently that everyone gets tangled up on his first try. Help him get disentangled and start again. Give him enough slack so that the lead is comfortable, but don't let it drag on the ground. Follow him wherever he goes. If he gets frightened and won't move, take a couple of steps yourself and call him. Don't pull on the lead. Coax him along with your voice. This session shouldn't last more than three to five minutes; repeat it once or twice a day for a couple of days, or until the puppy's completely used to the idea of moving around with a loose lead on. As soon as this is accomplished, you'll be ready to teach him what it's all about.

Snap the lead on his collar, and stand still. When he starts to move off, stay where you are and let him go out almost to the end of the lead. Now, squat down and call him back: "Puppy, come!" As he comes toward you, fold the lead up in your hands to shorten it. Don't let it trip him; you don't want to punish him for responding to your call. If he doesn't want to come (and why should he?), *don't yank*. For the time being, think of your lead as a thread that will break if you pull too hard. Give him a gentle tug each time you repeat the word "come." Stop tugging and praise him as soon as he comes toward you. When he gets to you, give him the Nobel Puppy Prize. Repeat the exercise for two or three minutes and knock off for the day.

Be sure to kneel or squat while you're doing all this. Your lead should be parallel to the ground or floor whenever you're giving him the signal to come. If you try it standing up, you'll only be tugging upward on the lead instead of giving your puppy a clear directional signal that he can understand and follow.

Don't start walking around with him on-lead until he's figured out this first exercise. When you do start walking him, call the puppy's name every time you change direction. This will attract his attention, and he'll probably see you change course and follow accordingly. If he doesn't, bend over, give his lead a gentle tug, and urge him along with your voice. Don't be lazy about bending over—you must get your hands down to the level of the puppy's collar to give him a clear signal. Jerking upward doesn't tell him anything. With gentle handling, lots of encouragement, and clear directional signals, your puppy should quickly learn to follow along with you on a slack lead. Don't worry about strict heeling yet. At this point you only want him to move along happily without dragging you or being dragged.

If your puppy won't move at all, don't pull him. Stop and ask yourself why he's resisting. If he's just plain sick and tired of the whole thing, don't push it. Take the lead off and try him again later. Incidentally, never schedule a training session right before or right after he's taken a meal because he'll be either too hungry or too full to pay attention. If he still won't move in your next session, he's either scared or being stubborn. In either case, don't try to move him with the lead. Don't tug at all. You'll either scare him still more or make him more resistant. Use your voice to get him going. If necessary, entice him with a toy or biscuit. Praise him lavishly as soon as he budges.

Every puppy will try to go barging off on his own from time to time, and he'll undoubtedly give himself a pretty good jolt when he hits the end of the lead. As soon as he picks himself up, call him toward you. Give him lots of praise as soon as he moves in your direction. Don't let him get into the habit of leaning against the collar and dragging you. As soon as he hits the end of his lead, call him back. If he doesn't respond, give him a quick jerk and lots of praise as soon as he stops pulling.

Your puppy may try to hold the lead in his mouth. He shouldn't. Take it out and start the exercise again. If he's just playing, he'll probably stop after a few corrections. If he doesn't, it may mean that his lead, snap, or collar is too heavy and should be changed. Or it may be that you're pulling too hard, and he's using his mouth as a shock absorber. Lighten up on your hands and equipment and go back to following him around on a loose lead for a few sessions. Every time he tries to take the lead in his mouth, tell him "No!" in your best melodrama-villain voice. Whenever he moves easily on a loose lead, praise him to the skies.

Never be afraid to go back to the beginning and start all over again if you run into trouble. This rule applies to every stage of training. From time to time, you will meet people who will suggest guaranteed gimmicks to cure any training problem you may have. Make up your mind right now to ignore them; they'll only waste your time and confuse your dog. There are no gimmicks in dog training, only basic principles. When you run into trouble, go back to them. You'll get better results in the long run.

Remember to keep your lessons short. No more than four or five minutes a session, and no more than two sessions a day. Your puppy has a very short attention span and tires quickly. Don't try to train him when he's sleepy or hungry.

Eventually, your puppy will realize that the most pleasant way to walk on-lead is close to you with a nice, comfortable, slack lead and lots of loving praise wafting around his ears. The more he tries to get away from you, the less pleasant his experience is going to be. He's bound to forget himself from time to time, but you'll be surprised how quickly he catches on. Even if he's a slow learner, be patient. It may take you a week or two, or even longer, to get your puppy to follow easily and happily on a loose lead. Don't rush it. You're going to be walking him for the rest of his life, and you can save yourself a lot of knock-down, drag-out arguments (literally) by starting out slowly and carefully.

All this may seem a pretty pedantic approach to something as simple as taking your dog for a walk. If you want to skip the whole thing, just remember that private dog trainers make a very good living off people who can't control their dogs on the street. If your puppy is going to grow into a giant, I suggest you get the jump on him now while he's still small enough to control easily. Furthermore, your dog's collar and lead are the basic tools you'll need for the rest of his training so you might as well learn to handle them properly in the beginning. Finally, lead training will be your puppy's first formal lesson. The rapport that you establish with him now will last throughout his training.

Most early puppy training should resemble playtime as much as possible. Even lead training should be fun for him. The rest of it should be fun for you. Get down on the floor with him. Snuggle him, tickle him, roll him around, throw his toys (especially if you want him to retrieve in later life), let him chase you. Get him used to hearing his name, being handled in any position, and impress him with the fact that you are a thoroughly lovable person to be with.

While we're on the subject of recreation, I should mention toys. Don't give your puppy old shoes or clothing to play with. You can't expect him to know the difference between the shoes you give him and the ones in your closet. If he chews things to shreds, don't give him rubber toys with squeakers. He'll only swallow the squeaker and eat the rubber, both of which can make him pretty sick and even kill him. Stick to old tennis balls—these are much sturdier than dog's balls from the pet store—shinbones, rawhide toys, and nylon bones.

Puppies love fighting games, and your little killer will undoubtedly pretend to attack you ferociously. This is perfectly normal, affectionate play. He will, however, bite down too hard from time to time, and I don't have to tell you how sharp those baby teeth are. Whenever he nips too hard, give him a sharp "No!" and let your hand go limp in his mouth. Don't snatch your hand away. If you do, he'll only instinctively grab for it. If he doesn't respond to your voice, give him a quick, smart tap under the chin with two fingers of your free hand. (If you *must* give him a pop from time to time, never hit him from above; this will only make him hand shy. If you give him a quick slap under the chin, he won't know where it came from.) Praise him the moment he lets go. All canines, wild and domestic, learn bite inhibition by biting too hard in play and being corrected by an angry playmate. This is an important lesson for your puppy. Don't make the mistake of roughhousing with gloves on; this will only develop a hard mouth and dangerous play habits.

In general, you should avoid any overt punishment while your dog is still a young puppy. Hitting him will only make him shy. Screaming will terrorize him or make him immune to verbal reprimands. Since he's too young for punishment, but old enough to acquire bad habits, your best bet is to keep him out of situations where he has an opportunity to misbehave; keep him off your best rugs, away from your best furniture, and out of trouble. Your kitchen is probably the most puppy-proof room. Put him in it when you can't supervise him. Don't leave lights or appliances plugged into outlets near the floor where your puppy can chew on the wires. Don't leave poisons in cabinets near the floor. You may not always remember to shut the doors.

This doesn't mean that he should spend *all* his time in the kitchen; obviously he needs to explore and socialize as much as possible. Just try to be sure that he relieves himself before you let him loose in civilized territory. If he climbs onto the furniture, and you plan to keep him off it in later life, keep him off now. This means keeping him off your lap while you're sitting on the furniture. No puppy can understand the difference between lying on your lap while you're sitting on the sofa and lying on the sofa by himself. If you want to hold him, sit on the floor.

Keep an eye on him while he's loose. The minute he misbehaves, give him a sharp "No!" Then call him to you, praise him for coming, and distract him with a toy or romp. If he doesn't come, go get him, and distract him. If you think this sounds like teaching a toddler to keep his fingers out of the ash trays, you're right.

Don't think that you can turn a young puppy loose in your house and ignore him. Trouble starts when bored puppies go looking for it. Remember, if he can't play with you, he'll find something else to do. In the event that you want to sit down in your own living room and have a normal conversation with a human being for a change, put the puppy in the kitchen. You're entitled to a little time of your own. Just keep him out of harm's way.

HOUSEBREAKING
3

Now comes the crunch. Your puppy is about three months old, and you're sick and tired of cleaning up after him. No other aspect of dog training is as fraught with anxiety and frustration for the novice dog owner as housebreaking. Yet it's basically a simple idea that, with a little patience and consistency, can be imparted to any dog.

First of all, let's consider the kind of behavior you expect from a house dog. If you have a small breed that rarely leaves your house or apartment, or if your own schedule prohibits regular outdoor walks, you'll want your dog to use a small, papered area of your house. If you live in the suburbs or out in the country, you'll want him to go outdoors, possibly to a designated area of your yard. If you live in a big-city high-rise, your dog will have to wait until he gets to the gutter. All this comes under the general heading of housebreaking and is derived from two basic principles of canine behavior: a dog is a creature of habit and he will not normally foul his own nest. Housebreaking is, therefore, simply a matter of habit building by means of regularly scheduled confinement and exercise.

Up until now your dog has slept in his crate or bed with constant access to a papered area. By the time he's three months old, he should be able to get through the night without having to relieve himself. He may not actually be doing it, but he should be physically capable. If you're in doubt about this, wait another week or two before starting your house training.

Paper training is probably the simplest method of housebreaking. If up until now your puppy has been carefully supervised and confined to a papered room at night and while you're out, he's almost paper-trained already. However, you'd undoubtedly like to reduce the size of the papered area and teach him to use it all by himself when he needs to. Begin by setting up a strict feeding schedule. And I mean *strict*. By the clock. Let's say 7:30 A.M., 1 P.M., and 8 P.M. if you're home during the day. Or 7:30 A.M., 6 P.M., and 10 P.M. if you work. This, of course, assumes your dog is getting three meals a day. If he's only getting two, serve them about twelve hours apart. If he's getting four, make sure the last meal is at least an hour before bedtime. In any case, set up a schedule that you can reasonably expect to stick to; i.e., one that won't be thrown off if you get stuck in traffic on the way home from work. Be serious about this. What goes in at regular hours will come out at regular hours.

Begin your paper training in the evening. Give your puppy his last food and water at least an hour before bedtime and be sure he relieves himself completely before turning in. Put him in his crate with some of his toys and shut the door. (Don't give him any rawhide, however. It will make him terribly thirsty, and he won't be getting any water until morning.) If you don't have a crate, you'll have to confine him to his bed by some other means. Some people put the puppy's bed in a closet with a baby gate across the door. Some shut him in the bathroom. However, it has to be a pretty small bathroom, otherwise he'll relieve himself at one end and sleep at the other. Besides, most dogs really hate being shut in the bathroom. Tying the puppy up should be your last option; a puppy can easily get tangled up and injure himself trying to get loose. If you absolutely must tie him, take him into your bedroom where you'll hear him if he gets into trouble. Don't tie him if you expect to leave him alone while you go to work.

The point of all this is to confine the puppy to an area where he won't want to relieve himself. I have found a dog crate to be the safest, most convenient means of doing this, and I strongly recommend that you invest in one. Your puppy will be spending a great deal of time in bed while he's being housebroken, and no dog wants to be shut off in a closet or bathroom while the rest of the family is busy somewhere else in the house. Even when he's not actually playing with you, he likes to be where the warm bodies are. A collapsible crate can easily be moved from kitchen to family room or bedroom, so the puppy can have company even when he's confined.

A lot of novice dog owners resist the idea of crating their dogs, and they all have well-meaning friends who accuse them of keeping their pets in a cage. If anyone gives you any grief, remind him that human babies are kept in cribs and playpens, and no one accuses their parents of cruelty. You are not being cruel; you are house-training your dog by the most humane and sensible method I know. It is the method used by virtually every professional breeder, handler, and trainer I've ever met, and I've never met a pro who couldn't housebreak a dog. Furthermore, your dog won't need a crate forever. By the time he finishes teething, you'll probably be able to sell it or put it away until you get your next puppy. Until then, make life a little easier on yourself and your dog.

After you've confined the puppy to his bed for the night, take up all the papers except the ones you want him to use. Leave the papered area large enough for him to take a few steps without missing. You can reduce it later after his aim improves. Set your alarm for bright and early, and get some sleep yourself.

When you wake up the next morning, don't go into the kitchen until you're ready to let the puppy out. There's no point in getting him prematurely excited. When you do let him out of his bed, carry him to his newspapers. Keep him on them until he performs. When he does, tell him you've never seen anything so adorable in your life. Then clean up, give him his breakfast and water, and put him back in his crate while you pull yourself together.

After half an hour, take the puppy out of his crate and carry him to the papers again. If nothing happens, put him back in the crate for another fifteen minutes before trying again. If you still get no results, put him back for another fifteen minutes. Don't let him stand on the papers looking around blankly for more than ten minutes. And don't play with him while you're waiting for action.

The point of all this is to determine how long nature needs to take its course after each meal. In this way you'll know how long to leave him in his crate after feeding him. If he has to stand around on his papers for an hour before the mood strikes him, he'll only get confused. You want him to associate *going to* the papers—or the yard or street—whenever he feels the need. If he's already been hanging around there for an hour, the message he gets is that he can take care of business wherever he happens to be at the time.

As soon as the after-breakfast show is over, you can play with him for a while and then put him back in his crate until the next mealtime. If you're going to work, put him on his papers again before leaving just in case all this activity has inspired him. However, if nothing happens, don't worry about it. If you have to be on the job at the dot of nine, it has probably occurred to you by now that you'll have to get up an hour or so earlier than usual. A sacrifice, yes, but it won't last forever. Once your puppy's old enough to get along without a big meal in the morning, you'll be able to cut him down to one trip before leaving. He might even have the whole thing figured out for himself by then.

If you can't come home for lunch, try to get home from work as early as you can at the end of the day. No six o'clock movies and no after-work cocktails for the duration of housebreaking. As soon as you get home, repeat the morning ritual. Papers, food and water, crate, papers, and play. If you've left him alone all day, be sure to give him a good romp. Confinement doesn't mean neglect. Then put him back in his crate until his next meal—at least an hour before bedtime. Be sure he uses the newspapers before you shut him up for the night.

Congratulations. You've just survived your first day of housebreaking, and you probably haven't had a single accident.

For the first couple of days, carry the puppy from his bed to the papers and stay with him until he performs. Be sure to praise him lavishly when he does. On the third day you can open the crate and call the puppy over to the papers. If he stops before he gets to them, scoop him up quickly, and put him on them.

As I've said before, dogs are creatures of habit. By this time, your puppy should be in the habit of using newspapers simply because he's had little or no opportunity to use anything else. The trick now is to teach him to go to them when he needs to. A couple of weeks of confinement, supervision, and consistent scheduling should give reliable results. However, you won't be sure your puppy is ready to be left alone without confinement until you test him. Let him out of his bed in the morning and pretend to ignore him. If he starts to squat anywhere but on his papers, grab him fast. Then go back to calling and showing him for a couple of days before you try again. When he finally gets up in the morning, strolls over to his papers, and performs without the slightest suggestion from you, you've cleared the first hurdle.

Once he's passed this test a few times, you can start giving him more freedom. Stay with him, though. He's still not ready to be turned loose in the house while you go to work. If he makes a mistake, you'll need to be there to give him a sharp "No!" and hustle him onto his papers. If you can't watch him, put him back in his crate. Eventually the day will come when he wakes up in front of the TV set, goes down the hall through the second door on the right and into the kitchen to *find* his newspapers. When this happens, break out the champagne.

Once your puppy has figured out the paper routine with you there to watch him, you can start leaving him loose in the house, or kitchen, for short periods of time. This is assuming he isn't trying to chew up everything he can get his teeth into. If he is, you'll have to keep him crated whenever you're not there to supervise. This, too, will pass once his adult teeth have grown in.

Supervision and confinement will keep your puppy's mistakes to a minimum. There will be a few, however, and there may still be a few people left on this earth who will tell you to rub your dog's nose in them. Don't do it, no matter how angry you get. It's disgusting, and it doesn't work. The people who tell you to rub your dog's nose in his own feces are probably the same people who told you it was cruel to put him in a crate. People have funny ideas about cruelty. If you catch your puppy in the act, yell "No!" and get him onto his papers even if it leaves a trail across the rug; it's the only way. Remember, too, to praise him whenever you see him using his papers.

Puppies are sneaky, however, and you won't catch him every time. Every dog training book I've ever read advises the reader not to punish his dog after the fact. In general, they're right. It's no good screaming at him for something he can't remember doing. I'm not convinced that this applies to housebreaking, however. According to the books, if you come home from work and find a dried-up stool on the carpet, you're supposed to stoically clean it up and forget about it. Job may have had that kind of patience, but I don't. If there is such an item on your floor, your dog will know exactly how it got there. After all, he's never seen you do anything like that, and besides, all dogs know exactly whose calling card belongs to whom. So go get him. (Remember, you don't call him to you for anything unpleasant.) Carry him to the spot and show it to him. Point to it—don't shove his nose in it. "What's this [expletive deleted] on the floor here?" you might ask in your most disapproving tone. "That's disgusting. You bad dog." Don't hit him. Just let him know you're not amused. Then you can let him go and clean it up. And you can remind yourself that he probably shouldn't have been running around loose in the first place.

If you're one of those lucky folks with a back yard you can let your dog out in, your housebreaking program will differ from paper training only in that you'll be developing an outdoor habit rather than a paper habit. The same principles apply: consistent scheduling, confinement, and praise.

Put your puppy's crate in a room with a door opening onto your yard; this will probably be the kitchen. Be sure that he relieves himself completely before going to bed and then shut him in his crate for the night. Leave a path of newspapers between the puppy's crate and the exit. I shouldn't have to tell you why.

The next morning, carry the puppy from his crate to the area of the yard you want him to use. (If he's too big to carry, open the kitchen door, put his lead on him, and *run* to the spot you have in mind.) Put him down and stay with him until his mission is accomplished. Praise him, bring him in, give him his breakfast, and put him back in his crate for about half an hour while you pry your eyes open. Then carry him out again. If nothing happens in ten minutes, bring him back. He's likely to find the great outdoors terribly interesting and terribly distracting. Unless the need is urgent, he'll have no idea why you brought him out there. You want him to learn that these trips to his special corner of the yard are strictly for business. If he just goes out and wanders around, take him back inside and try again fifteen minutes later. If you still don't get results, take him back in again.

Once you've learned how long it takes nature to call after each meal, you'll be able to make one trip. After his second visit to the yard, you can play with him for a while and then put him back in his crate until the next mealtime, when you'll repeat the whole damn thing all over again.

Be sure to carry or lead him to his appointed spot for the first couple of days. This will put the idea into his head before he starts getting confused by his own mistakes. By the third day, he should be ready to make it under his own steam with a little encouragement from you. Be sure to open the kitchen door *before* opening the crate. Then call the puppy and get him to follow you outside. Run if you have to. Keep him moving until he gets to his spot. If he stops, pick him up and carry him the rest of the way.

After a few days of this, you can try letting him out of his crate before you open the door. If he doesn't let go while you're fumbling with the latch, you're well on your way to housebreaking your dog. Once you're sure he can wait for you to open the door, you can start removing the newspapers. Leave the ones right in front of the door for last. There may still be days when he's quicker than you are.

Even after your puppy has learned to head for the door, wait for you to open it, and trot off to his corner of the yard almost automatically, be sure to accompany him on all his excursions. If you don't, he may forget why he went out, come back without having done it, and remember when it's too late.

Once he seems to have the idea, you can start letting him have longer and longer periods of supervised freedom in your house. Then you can start leaving him alone. (If he goofs, go back a step in your training for a few days and then try him again.) Remember to keep a strict schedule. If you have a nice handy yard, it's very tempting to just open the door and let him out every hour or so. This won't housebreak him. He has to learn to restrain himself indoors, and the only way you can teach him is by keeping him indoors.

City apartment dwellers have the most difficult housebreaking task of all; their dogs have to learn that their houses include not only their apartments, but their halls, elevators, lobbies, and sidewalks as well. So if you live in a high-rise, be prepared for a few embarrassing moments. Your dog is not going to make all his mistakes in the privacy of his own home.

The first thing you'll need is an urban dog-walking kit; i.e., a shopping bag containing a roll of paper towels, some plastic bags, and a can of spray disinfectant. Hang it over the front doorknob and take it with you whenever you take your dog out. Your routine will be the same as that of paper trainers and suburban housebreakers. Confinement and scheduling are basic. The evening before you make your first trip to the street, make sure the puppy completely relieves himself before you shut him up for the night. Then remove all the newspapers from the floor. The next morning, put the puppy's lead on him and carry him down to the street. Try to find a spot with little traffic and no parked cars. Next to a fire hydrant is usually the best. Put the puppy down in the street and wait for the miracle to happen. It probably won't take long. One of the advantages we city dog owners enjoy is the fact that our streets are highly stimulating. So many other dogs will have visited the same spot that yours is bound to get the point.

If your back will stand it, carry your puppy to the street for the first few days. This won't prevent *all* future accidents, but at least you'll be starting him out on the right foot. Inevitably, however, you're going to have to teach him to make it to the street on his own four feet. You won't have immediate success, so don't forget your clean-up kit. Your puppy is bound to forget himself in the elevator or lobby sometime, and you're going to have to clean it up right then and there. It's not the doorman's job. It's not the janitor's job. It's your job, so do it. To make matters worse—and you might as well expect the worst—the lady from apartment 4G who wants to have dogs banned from the building will undoubtedly arrive on the scene at the very moment your puppy is disgracing you. And if you think that's bad, your little darling will probably try to perform phase two of the operation while you're mopping up phase one. Yell "No!" and hope for the best.

Don't put the puppy up for sale yet. Even this will pass. Having suffered through it myself, let me offer a few tips: Ring for the elevator *before* taking the puppy out of his crate. It's the waiting around that gets you every time. If you're blessed with the last vestige of bygone elegance, an elevator man, ask him to wait while you get the puppy. If you have a self-service elevator, wait for it to arrive and leave your shoe in the door while you get the puppy. Open his crate, put his lead on him, and *run* to the elevator. Crowd him into a corner and, if possible, make him sit down. Talk to him. You might even bring a biscuit or toy. Anything to keep his mind off his problem. If he starts to squat in the elevator, pick him up. When you get to the lobby, run all the way to the street. If he stops, don't drag him. Pick him up quickly and carry him the rest of the way.

If your dog is too heavy to lift, you'll have to be clever. Crowd him into a corner or against a wall whenever you have to stand still. Whenever you move, run. And don't go out without your clean-up kit.

Until your dog has developed a reliable habit of heading off into the gutter whenever he feels the need, walk him in the street. If the traffic is too heavy, keep him walking between you and the curb, as close to the edge as you can. As soon as he starts to squat, shove him gently into the street.

A word about sidewalks. They are for people. Any puppy will make a few mistakes on the sidewalk. Any dog owner who fails to clean them up should be made to walk through them barefoot. The same goes for crosswalks and areas directly in front of building entrances. If you can't clean it up, at least shove it into the street. Use your foot, if necessary. Better your shoe than some antidog nut's.

No matter which house-training method you adopt, stick to a strict feeding, confinement, and exercise schedule for about two weeks. By then your puppy's digestive system should be functioning on a predictable basis, and he should be ready to start rejoining the human race. Keep an eye on him, however. Stay with him when he's running loose in the house, and confine him at night and while you're away for at least two more weeks. By the end of a month, you can start testing him alone. If he fails, go back to crating him a little longer.

Your dog will let you know when he has the whole thing figured out. He'll make it to the newspapers all by himself, or he'll go to the door and scratch or bark to get out. A few clever fellows will even bring you their leashes if you're slow on the uptake.

Whenever your puppy makes a mistake, it's usually your fault. You've let him run around unsupervised, you've let his feeding and exercise schedule come apart, or you've expected too much of him too soon. In every case, go back a step in your training for a couple of days and firm up your scheduling. When you first start to leave the puppy uncrated while you're out, confine him to the kitchen. He can't do as much damage there. If you come home and find a present on the floor, let him know how disappointed you are and plan to crate him the next time you leave. As he begins to figure it out, you may discover that he can safely be left loose for three hours—but not six hours. So crate him or not, according to how long you'll be gone.

After your puppy has shown you that he can be trusted alone in the kitchen, you can decide whether or not to let him have the run of the house while you're away. It's up to you. A great many adult dogs are routinely confined to a single room while their owners are out, and they don't seem warped in the least.

It's almost impossible to put a time limit on housebreaking. Some dogs pick it up right away. "Oh, not in the house? Fine." Others seem to be just plain stubborn, stupid, or dirty. With them it takes longer, but there is no reason why the above methods shouldn't work on any normal dog. I think it's reasonable to say that any dog that isn't reliably housebroken by the age of six months has a problem—and his problem is probably you. If you don't seem to be getting anywhere, review your methods. If you're sure you're doing everything right and still getting no results, see your vet. It may be that your dog has a physical problem that makes it difficult or impossible for him to restrain himself for normal periods of time. However, if he can hold it in a crate, he can hold it in your house.

If your dog soils his crate or bed when you first begin housebreaking him, it probably means that he hasn't developed the muscular control he needs to get through the night or working day. This is assuming, of course, that you haven't left him in his crate for fourteen hours. No dog can do the impossible. If you don't care enough about your dog's comfort to get up early or come straight home from work, don't have one. However, if your puppy has relieved himself before going to bed and still can't last seven or eight hours, clean his bed or crate thoroughly and put off housebreaking for another week or so.

The chances of a mature dog persistently soiling his crate are extremely slight, but such rare cases do occur. If your dog is one of these, you'll have to keep him in a papered room at night and whenever you go out. Since he lacks the normal sense of cleanliness that enables us to housebreak dogs, you're going to have a long, difficult job on your hands. You may even have to resort to the use of infant or children's suppositories to get him to perform on schedule. Even then, you may never be completely successful. These are very rare cases, however. Don't let this be your excuse for failing to housebreak a normal dog.

Many people, particularly city dwellers, like to combine paper and outdoor training. That way, you don't have to take your dog outdoors when one of you has a 104° F. temperature. If you can't get home from work at your regular hour, you can leave papers down for your dog and know that he won't explode before you can get him out. If you want to do this, paper-train your puppy first.

Use the system described earlier in this chapter. After he's reliably paper-trained, start all over again and teach him to go outdoors. Crate him for the night and take up all the papers. Take a sheet of newspaper with you when you take him out in the morning. If he absolutely refuses to relieve himself outdoors, put the paper down on the ground and let him use that. Then take him inside, play with him for a while, and crate him until his next trip. This time, take a smaller sheet of newspaper if he still needs one. Keep reducing the size of the newspaper until he's made the transition. Do not leave soiled newspapers in the street. Basically, you'll be housebreaking your dog twice. You may think it's a lot of trouble, but the first night he has diarrhea, you'll be glad you did it.

Let me conclude this chapter by relating a conversation I had not long ago with a professional dog trainer.

"What's the most common problem you get called in on?" I asked.

"Housebreaking."

"What do you do about it?"

"I put them on a strict schedule, have them confine the dog at night and while they're away, and get them to supervise him while he's running around the house."

"No gimmicks?"

"No gimmicks."

"That's so easy. Why do they have problems?"

"In most cases, the owners are just plain lazy."

"What do you do about that?"

"I charge them two hundred and fifty dollars."

If you're too lazy to housebreak your dog by the book, start saving your pennies.

4 CIVILIZING

If you ignore everything else in this book, remember what's on this page because it covers your basic approach to training and will apply to every lesson you teach your dog.

It has often seemed to me that people who have trouble with their dogs fall into one of two categories: those who praise but seldom punish, and those who punish but seldom praise. To be a successful dog trainer, you must do both. It's easy enough to remember to punish your dog when he misbehaves because you're usually angry at the time. However, punishment should never be simply an expression of your anger. Don't punish your dog—*correct* him. Stop him from doing what you don't want him to do. Then immediately get him to do something you do want and praise him for it. The double whammy. It goes like this:

You spot your puppy chewing his way through an electric light cord.

"No!" you yell. "Get away from there!"

He drops the cord and looks at you in amazement. Now, while you've got his attention, lay on the double whammy:

"Puppy, come." Call him nicely. You're not going to punish him, because he's already stopped misbehaving. When he gets to you, praise him and play with him a little.

Now, let's look at what you've accomplished. First, you've stopped him from chewing; then, by calling him, you've taken his mind off the light cord; and finally, you've praised him for doing something else. That's how the double whammy works. I think lab-coat types call it negative and positive reinforcement.

A purely negative approach (just screaming "No!" when you catch him at the light cord), if it works at all, will eventually saddle you with a sullen, browbeaten dog. If your dog is going to accept his training happily, he must learn that there are all kinds of goodies in store for him when he behaves well. A purely positive approach—calling and praising without yelling "No!"—will distract him for the time being but won't convey the message that electric light cords are off limits. You'll end up with a very affectionate, spoiled dog, if he doesn't electrocute himself first.

Dogs don't understand long lectures in deportment. They need sharp, impressive corrections *at the moment* they misbehave, and glowing praise as soon as they respond. The double whammy applies to every lesson from household rules to advanced obedience work, so don't forget it.

I suppose there are dogs in this world who figure out the rules of human society all by themselves and grow to a dignified old age without ever chewing up a sofa, stealing a roast beef, or making sexual advances at the knees of their owners' stuffiest dinner guests. I've never had a dog like that, and you probably won't either. By the time you get housebreaking pretty well under control, you'll be faced with a whole new set of problems. The first will undoubtedly be destructiveness.

Your puppy's baby teeth will begin to fall out in his fourth or fifth month. The new set should be completely in by his sixth month, although the toy breeds sometimes take a little longer. Incidentally, don't worry if he swallows his baby teeth. His digestive system can handle them. It can probably handle your mattress stuffing as well. All puppies need something to chew on when they're teething. See to it that yours has a rawhide toy or a nice big shinbone to work on. Don't let him have any kind of bone that might splinter. If he doesn't have something of his own to gnaw on, he'll look for something of yours.

Most dogs who get into the habit of chewing up furniture, books, and your favorite shoes usually start while they're teething and keep it up out of habit. So, it's especially important that your puppy not be allowed loose in the house without supervision while he's teething. Even if he has his own toys, he's bound to want to try something different someday. So keep a look-out, and the minute he starts to nibble at a table leg, give him a sharp "No!" call him away, praise him, and give him something else to chew on.

This is a cinch if you're home all day and have nothing better to do than watch your puppy. We poor working stiffs have to think of something else. Remember the housebreaking rule: If you're not there to keep your dog out of trouble, then keep trouble away from him. If you don't have a chew-proof room to leave him in when you go out, crate him. Be sure to leave him a bone or rawhide toy to chew on. If his gums are bothering him, put a wet washcloth in the freezer and give it to him after it freezes hard. Keep the puppy crated or confined when you go out until he loses all interest in chewing up the household. This may mean a couple of weeks or a few months. My own dog—a four-footed shredding machine if there ever was one—was eight months old before he could be trusted alone in the house. Don't faint. Your dog shouldn't be that bad if you confine him while he's teething. I didn't, and I paid for it. When you think he's over it, start letting him loose alone for a couple of hours at a time. If he chews something, crate him for another week or so. If he passes the test, gradually start lengthening his periods of freedom.

If you come home and find that he's destroyed something, hold your temper. Remember, it does no good to punish your dog for something he's forgotten. You can try setting him up for a correction by sitting down in the room with the chewed item and waiting for him to attack it again. Then treat the situation exactly as if you'd just caught him at it. I should warn you, however, that if this trick works at all, it'll only work a couple of times. After that, he'll learn never to chew anything while you're watching.

If you want to, you can try showing the puppy the thing he's chewed and tell him "No!" This may make *you* feel better, but it won't have a profound impression on your dog. At best, it may teach him to keep his teeth off that particular item, but he can always find something else. Your best bet is to keep your puppy away from chewable objects whenever you're not there to protect them. Unless he's a perfect monster, he'll probably forget about chewing once his adult teeth are in.

If your dog continues chewing, or takes it up, long after he's stopped teething, you have a different problem—probably boredom. In this case, you'll have to confine him when he's alone and give him plenty of attention and exercise when you're home. Persistent chewing is usually a symptom of restlessness.

You may also have a spite chewer; whenever he's angry or upset about something, he goes to work. This type is very selective in his choice of objects. He'll mangle your tennis racket because you don't take him to the courts with you, or your briefcase because you don't take him to work. If he's mad at you for something less specific, he'll demolish your bed. Treat a spite chewer like any other destructive dog and try to remember that he only does it because he loves you.

You might try some of the antichewing sprays they sell in pet shops. The problem here is that, unless you spray your whole house, you won't know what to spray until after your darling has chewed it. However, if you find one that works, and not all of them will, you can use it on your kitchen table legs, woodwork, or any other vulnerable object in your otherwise puppy-proof room.

CRYING

No dog likes being left alone at home. The best you can hope for is a reproachful look and a resigned sigh as you shut the door. Most puppies will cry the first few times you leave them. When yours starts to complain, give the door a good hard kick, yell "No!" and leave. He may start up again in a few seconds, but he won't be able to stay awake or interested long enough to keep it up. The best way to teach your dog to howl every minute you're away is to go back and comfort him every time he peeps. Don't think you're reassuring him; you're only teaching him that every time he yells, he gets what he wants—you.

If kicking the door doesn't work after a couple of days, try the next step: Wait outside for him to start crying. At the first whimper, fling the door open, march in, and yell "No!" If you want to make an even stronger impression, drop a large book flat on the floor with a bang. Then turn on your heel and leave without another word. Slam the door. This will probably shock the daylights out of your puppy. By the time he pulls himself together, he may well have forgotten all about crying. I don't blame you if you feel terrible the first time you do this, but don't give in. Repeat this procedure every time you leave until he quietly accepts your departure. The whole idea is to give him an unpleasant experience whenever he cries. You must nip this problem in the bud, or it will become a terrible nuisance and probably get you evicted.

Most adult dogs who persistently howl when left alone do it out of habit and boredom. I suspect that many of them entertain themselves with their own vocalizing. Whatever the cause, it's a pain in the neck. If you find yourself living with an adult howler, set aside a day off or a weekend to deal with the problem. Leave in the morning as if you were going to work. Wait for the first note of protest. Then throw the door open and lay on the performance I've described above. Wait outside for a minute or so. Before he starts to cry, go back inside and praise him to the skies for being such a sweet, quiet dog. Hang around for a few minutes and repeat the exercise. Keep it up all day if necessary, gradually lengthening the periods of time he's left alone. By the end of the day, he should get the message: Cry and get scolded, keep quiet and get praised. If he hasn't figured it out by nightfall, do it again the next day. Once he gets to the point where he'll keep quiet for half an hour or more, you'll probably have the problem licked. Most solitary howlers start the minute you leave and keep it up out of habit. It's the departure that triggers it. Once you get him over that hump, he'll probably forget about starting up later.

If this doesn't work, think about getting your dog a pet. Not another dog. You'll only make him jealous, and you might end up with *two* howlers. A cat, a canary, a hamster, even a turtle may provide just enough company to keep him quiet and will be a lot cheaper than your last resort—a dog sitter.

THAT'S *MY* CHAIR

You come home from a hard day at the salt mine to discover that your sheepdog has turned your new upholstery into a hair shirt. You remember that it does no good to correct him for something he's forgotten, so, cursing and grumbling, you drag out the vacuum cleaner and get to work. You *are* a good sport.

First of all, if you don't want your dog on the furniture, keep him off from the very beginning. This includes, as I've said before, never holding the puppy in your lap while you're sitting in your favorite chair. Up is up to him, and the fact that your lap may be separating him from the slipcovers means nothing. If you catch him climbing aboard, give him a nasty "No!" and get down on the floor with him. If you catch him snoozing on the sofa, tell him "Get off!" and put him on the floor. Get down there with him and play with him for a minute. Don't say "Get down." As you'll learn in the next chapter, "down" means "lie down," and he's already lying down—on the sofa.

Most dogs who are never allowed on the furniture don't think of getting on it all by themselves—especially if they have comfortable beds of their own. However, it often happens that some members of the family—let's blame it on the kids—allow the puppy on the furniture when you're not around. Or maybe you let him on the old sofa, and now you can't keep him off the new one. Whatever the reason, he thinks he has squatter's rights. He waits until you're out of sight, settles on the settee, and jumps off the second he hears you returning.

If you have one of these sneaky devils (and there are zillions of them), you can do one of three things: you can keep him as clean and well brushed as possible and learn to share; you can shut him in the kitchen with his own bed whenever you go out; or you can try the mousetrap gimmick. I've never used this trick myself, so I pass it along only as an untested suggestion. Set several mousetraps on your dog's favorite chair or sofa. Cover them with several layers of newspaper and tape the papers down securely. The idea is *not* to come home and find your dog walking around with a mousetrap on his toe. The theory is that when your dog gets on the sofa, he sets off the mousetraps, which snap against the paper making a noise that scares him off. That's the idea, and I hear it recommended all the time. Frankly, I'm a little suspicious of anything that gimmicky, and I can't imagine many dogs falling for it. Furthermore, nobody ever tells you what to do if it doesn't work. If you're going to go to all that trouble, why not throw an old blanket over the sofa and let him sleep there?

Your best bet is never to let him on the furniture in the first place. If he turns into a sofa sneak, put his bed in the kitchen and shut him in there whenever you go out. This has to be easier than mousetraps.

COPROPHAGY—DON'T ASK

Most dog owners are spared this problem, thank goodness. Stool eating is uncommon but by no means rare. No one knows exactly what causes it, but some vets suspect a nutritional deficiency. If you catch your dog eating stools, scold him and get him away. Have him checked for worms, put him on a vitamin and mineral supplement if he doesn't already get one, and add an occasional helping of raw liver to his dog food.

This isn't an easy habit to break, so try not to let it get started. While your puppy is still using newspapers, be sure to clean up as soon as you can after each performance. Puppies will play with anything. A mature dog who eats stools should not be paper-trained and left alone all day. You'll have to train him to go outside and keep him away from temptation as much as possible. If he spends a lot of time outdoors in a run by himself, get a pooper scooper and use it religiously. Supervision and cleanliness are the only real help. You might also consult your vet about a diet supplement that will make your dog's stools unpalatable—and I hope you appreciate the humor of this concept.

The above problems crop up most frequently with dogs who are left alone much of the time. Dogs are sociable creatures; they do not like solitude. Don't think that just because you have a nice big house or yard for your dog to run around in, he'll be happy in it all by himself. When you're not there, he probably won't even get off his duff to run around except to get into trouble. However, very few of us can stay home all day to keep our dogs company. If you have to leave your dog alone while you go out to work, consider this—he'll be less lonely, less bored, and less likely to misbehave if he's sleeping. And he's not going to sleep while you're at work if he does nothing but sleep while you're at home. Even dogs can't sleep twenty-four hours a day.

What I'm getting at is this: If you leave your dog alone for several hours a day, you *must* see to it that he gets plenty of exercise and attention while you're home. You can't spend all day at work and all night in front of the television without your healthy, lively dog getting very bored and very restless. That's how trouble starts.

Make time for your dog. This might mean getting up an hour earlier to give him a good run in the park before you go to work. Or it might mean giving up a few reruns to get him out on summer evenings. Even a toy breed needs a good workout on the floor every day. This is the only real cure for the boredom and restlessness that lie at the heart of most absent-owner training problems. A little exercise wouldn't hurt you any, either. Furthermore, if your dog has to be confined to a kitchen or a crate temporarily while you're out earning his dog food, he won't mind it as much if he's well exercised. He might even welcome a few hours' rest.

BLOCKS AND TACKLES

Unless your dog is a real featherweight, you probably won't want him jumping up on everyone he meets. From your dog's point of view, jumping on people is just a display of affection. Unfortunately, people in white linen suits aren't likely to see it the same way. Furthermore, such gestures are totally unappreciated by people who are afraid of dogs.

To begin with, if you don't want your dog to jump on other people, don't let him jump on you. You probably don't mind it, but he can't make the distinction. So put a stop to jumping, period. If you want to give your dog a great big hug and a kiss—and why shouldn't you? bend over.

There are two sure ways to teach a dog not to jump on you. If he's a large dog, lift your knee against his chest or tummy as he jumps. Don't kick him. Just lift your knee. After he jumps into it a few times, he'll figure the whole thing out. If you have a little dog, step gently on his hind feet. Don't stamp. Apply just enough steady pressure to make him back off.

If your dog decides to throw himself into the arms of everyone who comes to your house, snap a lead on him before you open the door. As soon as he jumps, give him a sharp jerk backward and make a few nasty remarks. Don't drag him away. Jerk hard enough to make a serious impression and then release. Let him approach your guest again on a slack lead, and praise him as long as he keeps four feet on the ground. If he forgets himself and jumps again, correct him again. Keep your voice low and calm while you're praising him. Don't excite him any more than necessary. After a few lessons in front-door courtesy, he'll get the message.

While we're on the subject of dogs jumping on people, we might as well cover the sexual experimentations of male puppies. There are few things more embarrassing than finding your darling boy with his forelegs clamped around your missionary aunt's knee going through all the motions of passionate lovemaking. Try not to have nightmares about it; it happens to everybody. When males reach or approach sexual maturity, they experience a lot of strange new urges and have no clear idea where to direct them. So they try sofa cushions, the cat, you, anything that happens to be handy. However, there's a time and a place for everything. Pull him off Aunt Nellie and let him know in no uncertain terms that well-brought-up fellows don't go in for that kind of thing. Children, because they roughhouse with dogs much more than adults do, are frequently the objects of such advances. Explain to your kids, in details of your own choosing, that such behavior is most unseemly, and teach them to correct the puppy whenever he loses his head.

Don't be afraid to be quite firm about this. Be permissive with your kids, if you want. They don't have dogs' libidos. Your puppy will never read Freud and will not become repressed if he has to learn to keep his paws to himself. The first offended out-of-season bitch he tries his technique on won't be half as gentle as you.

FEAST AND FAMINE

No healthy dog ever starved himself to death in his own home. Don't get into the habit of adding or substituting gourmet goodies just to get him to eat. If he turns up his nose at dog food today, he'll be that much hungrier for it tomorrow. If he persists in not eating, it's not his taste buds that are bothering him. Get him to the vet.

The only time you should really pamper your dog's appetite is when he's sick and refuses to eat. In that case, you should use every trick in the book to encourage him. Soak his food in gravy. Give him raw hamburger. Feed him by hand. Pretend to eat his food yourself and then share it with him. In a real emergency, give him anything remotely nourishing that you can get down him. I once met a bloodhound who had just about given up the ghost after being hit by a car. His owner kept him alive on a diet of coffee ice cream. He eventually recovered and went back to dog food, although he still got a little ice cream for dessert every now and then for sentimental reasons.

Some dogs will eat just enough to keep body and soul together but not enough to maintain a proper weight level. This is often true of large, lethargic breeds like Great Danes and Irish wolfhounds that need a lot of food but are too lazy to work up a healthy appetite. If this is your problem, exercise is the only answer. You'll have to get him out and running, and you'll have to go with him to keep him at it. Take him jogging. Get a bicycle and take him out for road work. Throw sticks and balls up and down hill for him. A friend of mine solves the problem by sending her Great Dane out to play with a flirtatious standard poodle bitch who runs him ragged. However, if you can't provide a playmate, you'll have to work him yourself. Don't think you can turn him out in the yard alone to do solitary calisthenics. If he were a self-starter, you wouldn't have this problem to begin with.

I have to admit that picky eaters aren't my specialty. Most of the dogs I've had ate everything in sight and had to be kept on perpetual diets. I had a dachshund once who put away an entire Christmas fruitcake while the rest of the family was out carolling. A pound of chocolates was just a snack to her. She was the most voracious eater, the most shameless beggar, and the most ingenious food thief I've ever met, but she kept her figure for sixteen years. If she'd had all the goodies she wanted, her life would have been a lot shorter.

If you've got a chow hound, be prepared to be cruel. Figure out how much food your dog needs to keep healthy and slim, and feed him just that amount every day. Use a measuring cup. Incidentally, beware of the feeding instructions on the dog-food package. I've found that the amounts they recommend are often too much for the average house pet.

Don't expect your dog to like this treatment. He'll plead, he'll complain, he'll threaten, and, when all else fails, he'll take up panhandling. Be tough, and tell the neighbors not to feed him no matter what he says.

First of all, build up an immunity to begging. Once your puppy learns that a soulful look—with his chin resting on your knee because he's so weak from hunger he can't hold his own head up—a cute trick, or a pitiful whine will get him an hors d'oeuvre, you're well on the way to having an overweight pest on your hands. So don't get into the habit of flipping him a peanut from every handful or passing down samples from the dinner table. If you want to give him table scraps, serve them with his dinner in *his own* dish. Also, keep a sharp eye on the kids. Foods children don't like have a way of getting under the table and into the dog.

If your dog can't con you into feeding him until he bursts, he may resort to desperate measures. Forget about training the confirmed food junkie not to steal. At best, you can discourage him from snatching food right off your plate or out of your mouth, but don't think you can leave a plate of cocktail sausages on the coffee table while you answer the telephone. Remember, too, that a kitchen counter is a coffee table to a Great Dane, and even a tiny food thief doesn't mind a little second-story work. My notorious dachshund once swiped most of the leftovers from the breakfast table. We knew she was the perpetrator because she left her toothprints in the butter, but we never did figure out how she got onto the table.

A normal to less-than-eager eater can, however, be taught not to steal without much trouble. At the same time, you can teach him a trick that will amuse your more impressionable guests. Put a tidbit on the edge of a low table and wait. As soon as your dog reaches for it, tell him "No!" If he doesn't respond, put him on lead and give him a jerk. Praise him as soon as he backs off. After he's waited quietly for a couple of minutes without grabbing, put the tidbit in his dish and let him eat it. Do this every time you're having a snack and after a couple of days he should get the idea that food on the table isn't his. By enlisting the help of any friends who drop by for coffee, you can use the same technique to teach him to refuse food from strangers. This isn't a bad lesson if you live in a high dognapping area.

Don't expect these lessons to work on a compulsive food freak; all he learns from this is not to steal food while you're watching. When you're not there to guard your goodies, lock them up, and don't leave the keys lying around.

DRIBBLING

Many dogs pass a little urine whenever they greet their owners or are reprimanded for something. Some even roll over on their backs and widdle, probably to be sure you won't miss it. This isn't really a housebreaking problem. In fact, many perfectly house-trained dogs do it. Actually, this behavior is an instinctive demonstration of extreme submissiveness. Your dog is letting you know in the clearest canine language he knows that he considers you the ultimate boss. If you've selected a puppy from the very bottom of the litter's pecking order, you can expect to see this kind of behavior from time to time.* The worst thing you can do in this case is to punish your dog. You'll only make him think he hasn't gotten his point across, so, naturally, he'll repeat himself. The bright side of this problem is that a very submissive dog doesn't need a lot of harsh reprimands but responds best to gentle corrections and positive praise.

If your dog dribbles when he greets you at the door, try to avoid strong entrances. Don't make a great fuss over him the second you arrive. Don't even look at him. A direct stare is a signal of dominance and can easily trigger a submissive response—right on the rug. Don't approach him or pat him. Just say "Hi," walk in, take off your coat, and sit down. Don't worry about hurting his feelings. He'll come to you by himself. By not flaunting your dominance, you'll reduce his need to show submission.

SIBLING RIVALRY

A couple of years after I was born, my parents' cocker spaniel moved out. She took up residence with a childless couple in the neighborhood and lived with them to a pampered old age. No hard feelings. She was just used to being an only child and wanted to keep it that way.

If you're planning to raise a family as well as a dog, I'd advise you to have a

* Dogs will also pass urine and even defacate in moments of extreme fear; but I'm assuming here that your dog isn't terrified of you and is only showing submission.

baby first. But who can be that organized? If you find yourself with a new baby and a dog who always considered himself your number one son, treat the situation much as if your dog were an older brother. Give him as much attention as your enchantment with your new offspring will allow. Introduce him to the baby gradually and don't insist that he love him right away. Don't be surprised if he, like many children, reverts to infantile behavior for a while. It's not unheard of for a mature model of deportment to chew up some furniture and desecrate a few carpets after a new baby arrives. If he behaves like a puppy, treat him like one. Confine him when you can't supervise, but don't neglect him. Getting shut off in a crate somewhere while the family gushes over the new baby won't help his attitude any. Keep him with you as much as possible, let him know that you love him as much as ever, but don't put up with any nonsense either. He'll probably snap out of it in a week or so, and the day may come when he growls at you for spanking your own kid. However, if it becomes clear that he's not going to adjust, find him a new, preferably childless, home before he takes his jealousy out on the baby. You can always get another dog.

You may decide to get a second dog someday. Your first dog will probably put up with just about any puppy you bring home. Even if he doesn't actually play with him, the worst he'll do is tell the youngster to mind his manners and stay out of the way. The puppy, being a puppy, will probably oblige. However, puppies grow up, and when yours starts feeling full of himself, you'll undoubtedly have a few squabbles to contend with. Don't worry about it. In general, your best bet is to let them work it out. You may have to treat a couple of bloody noses and bruised egos before the matter is settled, but eventually one dog will establish his dominance and the other will learn to accept the vice presidency.

There are a few things you can do to ease the conflict. Life will be much easier if your second dog is of the opposite sex from the first. Males and females will quarrel from time to time but rarely get into a serious fight. If you must have two of the same sex, try to find a puppy who will be clearly submissive (preferable) or clearly dominant to your older dog when he grows up. (All puppies are submissive to older dogs. You'll have to judge his potential adult submissiveness or dominance by his relationship to his brothers and sisters in the litter.) Within litters and wolf packs, the most frequent and serious scraps occur between animals who are close together in the pecking order. Number one fights with number two, number four fights with number five, but number five rarely talks back to number one. So if you can be flexible enough in your training to handle two different personality types, you can try this approach.

Whatever you do, be aware of the dangers of trying to integrate two aggressive, dominant dogs of the same sex into your family—particularly terriers and members of the large sporting and working breeds. If you have to keep two dogs separated all the time, you'll end up with two half-pets, which is no substitute for one whole one. So don't be greedy.

After all that moralizing, I have to admit that another puppy is often hard to resist. If you do give in to temptation, don't neglect your first dog when you bring your puppy home. Give him lots of attention for the first few days. If he has a favorite member of the family, try to discourage his favorite from making a great fuss over the puppy.

If your second dog is a full-grown one, try to arrange to have the two dogs meet somewhere away from home—away from both homes. They'll feel less compelled to fight on neutral territory and have a chance to get acquainted before anyone's home turf is violated. This may ease the situation enough for the second dog to settle in without a serious hassle. In any case, two dogs who have to live together should be allowed a few snaps and growls while they sort out their relationship. If you interfere too much, you'll only postpone the rapprochement.

This does not apply to two dogs who *don't* have to live together. Your dog should not be allowed to make insulting remarks to every stranger he passes on the street. If he shows signs of becoming a scrapper, put a stop to it right away. The only really safe way to stop a dog fight is to prevent it. Watch your dog as he approaches another. Do his legs and back stiffen? Does the hair on his back stand on end? Is his tail vibrating stiffly? Any of these signs indicates that he's in a challenging mood. This doesn't mean he's going to hurl himself at another dog's throat, only that he's prepared to. He may sniff, exchange vital statistics, and relax. Or he may not. Be ready to grab him just in case.

Some dogs fight only in their own yards, and some go out looking for trouble. Some are terrors when they're on-lead and pussycats when they're off. Some never curl a lip. Until you're sure your dog is a pacifist, be alert when he approaches another dog of the same sex. On the other hand, don't be too quick to snatch him away. He's got to learn to handle his own social life someday. Just stay on your toes and be ready to bail him out if you have to.

Don't think that because your dog was a friendly puppy, he'll be a friendly adult. All puppies are friendly. You won't know for certain how he'll handle himself until he's over a year old. Meanwhile, get him acquainted with most of the neighborhood dogs while he's still a pup. You might even take him to kindergarten. Many dog clubs hold puppy-training classes that include regular socializing sessions so the puppies can get to know strange dogs and people, and get used to being around them.

If he gets into the habit of taking a swing at other dogs while he's on-lead, recruit some friends with quiet dogs to help you set him up for a correction. Have your friend hold his own dog still on a short lead. Approach him with your own dog on a slack but short lead; i.e., loose enough so that he's comfortable, but short enough so that he can't deviate from his course by more than a few inches. Talk nicely to him as you approach your friend's dog. "Come on, puppy. Let's go. Good boy." The second he starts his dive at the other dog, give him a very sharp jerk, a nasty "No!" and walk away. As soon as he's taken his attention off the other dog, start sweet-talking him again. "Come on, boy. Forget about it. Let's go." Don't drag him away. Give him a series of jerks if necessary, but give a release after each jerk.

Now, circle around and repeat the lesson again. After a few passes, he should be able to get by the other dog without blinking. When he does, give him the Nobel Peace Prize. Now go home and call up another friend and repeat the whole thing again the next day with another dog. Don't consider this a cure for fighting. It's only a lesson in street manners. If he's a real terror, you're going to have to keep him on-lead whenever there are strange dogs around. If you must let him run loose for exercise, put a muzzle on him.

In the event that your dog ever gets into a real battle, for heaven's sake, don't wade into the middle of it. A fighting dog is in such a frenzied state that he'll bite anything in front of him, even his owner. Two people can separate fighters by each grabbing one dog's hind legs or tail and pulling them apart. However, even your own dog may snap at you when you try this. If you have the strength to do it, grab his hind feet, spin around quickly, and literally throw him behind you. By the time he picks himself up, he'll probably have come to his senses.

Many trainers suggest throwing a blanket over fighters, throwing firecrackers at them, or turning a hose on them. These are excellent suggestions if you happen to have a blanket, firecracker, or hose handy. Unfortunately, many professional trainers make the same mistake everyone else does when a fight starts—they wade in, grab a dog, and get bitten. Incidentally, don't try beating them. The pain you inflict will only incite them to fight harder. I realize that it's just about impossible to keep your cool when it looks as though your dog is getting killed right in front of you, but try. In most fights, the loser gives up well short of death's door, and the winner stops fighting as soon as he sees the surrender flag. There's no point in both of you getting chewed up. The vet bill will be stiff enough. So unless you really think a dog is going to be killed, or you're absolutely sure you can handle the situation without being badly bitten—obviously, you can break up a Chihuahua fight without losing more than a finger or two—let 'em fight. If this seems hard on your dog, remember that you shouldn't have let it get started in the first place. This applies both to you and the no-good rotten creep who let his dog attack yours.

ADOLESCENT NERVES

At the age of four or five months, your heretofore fearless puppy may seem to turn into a cringing neurotic. He may be afraid to go into a room where you've switched the furniture around. The sight of a strangely dressed person may throw him for a loop. Peculiar sounds may send him up the wall. At this age, your puppy is experiencing what the canine behaviorists call environmental learning. Put simply, he's making a mental record of his surroundings and figuring out where he belongs. Any sudden environmental change, a sight or sound that doesn't fit the pattern he's used to, may upset and frighten him. A great many dogs show no sign of this at all, probably as a result of domestication and selective breeding. It's common to all wild canines, however, and seems to turn up most often in the larger breeds of domestic dog.

If your puppy should develop adolescent nerves, don't worry about it too much. He'll probably grow out of it. Try to avoid obviously frightening or unpleasant situations. Don't take him to fireworks displays, riots, costume parties, parades, etc. If you think a situation will frighten him, and it's not one that he *has* to get used to, stay away from it. Incidentally, don't take him through the car wash. It could put him off cars for years. Don't baby him either. This is no time for him to lead a sheltered life. Take him to your friends' homes, to stores that allow dogs, to parks. If you live in a city, take him for long walks. Whenever he seems frightened, reassure him. Encourage him to investigate strange objects. If he's afraid of something, approach it yourself. Touch it. Call him to you and show him that it's harmless.

You'll probably discover that your dog is most easily frightened by things that look like people or animals but aren't—like store dummies, coats on hangers, and stuffed toys. He'll also, much to your embarrassment, be afraid of people who don't look like people to him—someone carrying a large object, a person in a wheelchair, someone dressed strangely. I have a friend whose poodle flipped out when her husband walked in one night wearing a ski mask over his face. ("Flipped out" is putting it mildly. She jumped over the stove.)

As I said before, your dog may show none of these symptoms of environmental fear. Even if he does, he'll probably grow out of them with gentle handling. In any case, don't expect a high degree of sophistication when he's four to six months old.

PHOBIAS

Many dogs develop specific fears that stick with them throughout their lifetimes. Cousins of mine had a cocker spaniel who hated the local newspaper. She had no quarrel with the *New York Times* or the *Wall Street Journal*, but, given half a chance, she'd tear the *Red Bank Register* to shreds. It may have been that she hated one of the delivery boys and took it out on the paper. Whatever the reason, as my grandmother used to say, "That dog had no use for the *Register*."

Dogs are individuals, and they all have their quirks. Most of these are only slightly annoying, and their irritation is usually outweighed by the fun we have telling amusing stories about them. Some phobias can be serious, however. Among these, fear of thunderstorms is the most common. Many dogs hide under a chair and tremble until the storm has passed, and others become downright hysterical. In extreme cases, they may be seized by running fits. They crash into walls and furniture, they run right through screen doors, even picture windows. (Earthquakes, too, will trigger running fits, as any Californian will tell you.) If your dog becomes hysterical during thunderstorms, get your vet to prescribe a tranquilizer you can give him whenever a storm starts to build up. If he's a runner, throw a coat or blanket over him. This will make it easier for you to hold him still and protect you in case he bites. If he's too strong for you, leave him alone. Don't leave him in a screened porch or a room with glass doors or picture windows when you go out.

Fortunately, extreme reactions are pretty rare. Most dogs who notice thunderstorms at all are only moderately afraid. Be as quiet and reassuring as you can. Let him choose his own shelter, and let him wait it out. Don't baby him too much. After all, it's not going to hurt him.

He may be helped by the following treatment. Make a tape recording of a severe thunderstorm. Then play it while you play with your dog. Play it while he's eating dinner. Play it any time that something pleasant is happening to him. He may, in time, learn to associate the sound with pleasant experiences and thereby overcome his fear.

TRAFFIC HAZARDS

Car chasing is probably the most dangerous habit your dog can get into. It's also an extremely difficult habit to break. Cars seem to touch off an instinctive prey-catching response in some dogs and can make even the most obedient ones immune to command.

As soon as your dog shows an inclination to chase cars, set him up for a correction by letting him out and driving around the block in your car. Take a friend and a bucket of water with you. As soon as your dog starts to chase you, have your friend throw the water on him. Try it again the next day with your friend's car. Then get hold of another friend and do it again with still a different car. If a few good dousings don't work, don't fool around with the problem. You can either build a fence around your yard or tie your dog up. If you can't bear to do either of these, start saving your money for a new dog. This one won't last long.

As any newsboy will tell you, a lot of dogs can't stand the sight of a person on a bicycle. They chase them, bark at them, and sometimes take a few nips for the sheer thrill of it. If your dog is a bike freak, you'll have to set him up for a correction. Put him on-lead and take him to a park where there are a lot of cyclists or to an elementary school at three o'clock. If you can't manage this, recruit a friend with a bike. Station yourself in a spot where the cyclists will pass you, or have your friend ride past you a few times. As soon as your dog makes a dive for a bike, give him a sharp jerk and praise him as soon as he takes his attention off the bike. Repeat this for fifteen minutes or so every day until he consistently ignores passing bicycles.

Now you've taught him not to chase bikes while he's on-lead. Big deal. If he doesn't remember the lesson when he's loose, pass out water pistols to the neighborhood riders and tell them to give your dog a few squirts in the face whenever he chases them. If you're a cyclist, keep a water pistol for yourself. You never know when someone else's dog might chase you. If all this seems like too much trouble, try keeping your dog in his own yard where he belongs.

BITING

On meeting your dog for the first time a lot of people will ask, "Does he bite?" If your dog has ever shown the slightest tendency to snap at anyone for any reason, for God's sake, say "Yes." Prevention is the only cure for biting, and it doesn't cost you anything to have your dog treated with a little respect. Furthermore, in these difficult times, it doesn't hurt to have some people think you keep a nasty dog on the premises. Only you and your friends need know what a pushover he is.

All dogs bite—yours included. A dog who has never so much as growled may well bite if he's sick, injured, or badly frightened. He may become cranky and snappy with old age. A bitch with puppies may defend her litter with her teeth. A dog may even become mentally ill and dangerous. Very few people who have spent a lifetime working with dogs have never been bitten, although most of them will tell you that their bites resulted from their own carelessness or misjudgment. Don't let this frighten you into letting your dog bluff and browbeat you for the rest of his life. Just remember to respect him for what he is—a basically friendly animal whose natural defense is his teeth.

Although all dogs *can* bite, few will. Wolves, who finally seem to be getting the good press they deserve, have a powerful inhibition against biting their fellow pack members. By the same token, your dog regards, or should regard, you and your family as members of his pack, so he's not likely to bite you. Under normal circumstances, this inhibition will carry over to other humans as well. In fact, more than a few dogs fail attack-training courses precisely because they can't overcome their unwillingness to bite people.

Most people who are bitten by their own dogs in cases other than panic, injury, or illness have failed to establish social dominance over their pets. The dog has, in effect, become the owner's rival. Although rival dogs can be expected to exchange a few snarls and snaps before one of them submits to the other, dogs and humans shouldn't have to work out their relationships the same way. When I say that you should be dominant in your relationship with your dog, I don't mean domineering. You don't have to shove him around and shriek *"Achtung!"* every time you want him to do something. You do, however, have to assume and maintain a superior social position. Actually, this is easily, and often unconsciously, achieved. Most properly raised puppies accept human dominance with little argument.

You can see your own dog's submissiveness in the way he greets you and in the way he tries to make it up to you after he's misbehaved. When you come home from work, he meets you at the door with his tail high and wagging happily. His ears are up. His mouth is open in a friendly smile. He may rub or bump his head against you in an appeal for affection. These are all signs of active submission. In dog language, they mean "Hiya, boss."

Whenever you scold your dog, he tries to redeem himself with a display of passive submission. He lays his ears back, looks away sheepishly, and stretches his lips back horizontally in an embarrassed grin. His tail is tucked down and possibly vibrating nervously at the tip. If you touch him, he remains perfectly still or raises a forepaw beseechingly. If he thinks he's in real trouble, he may roll over on his back and even pass a little urine.

Some dogs anticipate a reprimand by apologizing before you know what they've done. You come home, and your dog greets you with a display of submission that would embarrass Attila the Hun. He's got guilt written all over him. It doesn't take a genius to guess that he's been rummaging through the wastebaskets again.

These are all signs by which a dog displays his deference to a superior dog or human. If your dog behaves this way for you, you know you've got the upper hand. If you don't have his respect, get it. Not with abuse, but with consistent, firm authority as well as plenty of affection. When you want to demonstrate your dominance to your dog, stand up straight—big dogs dominate little ones—look him right in the eye—staring is a dominant signal—speak in a firm, authoritative voice—like a warning growl—and don't take "No" for an answer. If you find it absolutely necessary to administer corporal punishment, give him a quick smart rap under the chin, or, if he's little enough, pick him up and shake him. Don't swat him with newspapers, and never hit him with his lead. This is a training tool, not a weapon.

At the same time, encourage his displays of submission. Reward his head bumping with a pat or a scratch behind the ears. If he rolls over on his back, rub his tummy. Let him know you're the nicest boss a dog ever had.

To get back to biting, since your own dog considers you the leader of the pack, the chances of his biting you out of pure defiance are practically nil. Nonetheless, he may, if he's the competitive sort, take a crack at bluffing you. Don't give in if he growls at you. Unless the growl is accompanied by other signs of aggression—staring, ears up, hackles raised, lip curled, legs and tail stiff—you're probably safe in considering this nothing more than a grumbling complaint. Tell him nobody talks to you in that tone of voice. Stare him down and tell him to get his fanny out of your chair this minute.

If your dog ever bites anyone at all, it will probably be a stranger. For this reason, it is extremely important that he have as many pleasant meetings with as many pleasant people as possible during the first year of his life—especially during the first six months. With this kind of socialization, a shy puppy can gain confidence, and an aggressive one can learn restraint.

Introduce your puppy to everyone who comes to your house, and take him with you to as many different places as you can. This is especially important if you live in a crowded city. A city dog is constantly confronted with people who have no idea how to approach a strange dog. They give him quick pats in passing. They reach over his head and snatch their hands away the second he raises his nose to see what they're doing. They let their kids run up and grab him without an introductory sniff. A sophisticated city dog has to learn to put up with all of this without getting frightened or defensive. The best time to teach him is when he's still a puppy and loves everything that moves.

If your dog does become snappy as an adult or gets crotchety in his old age, remember, he's your responsibility. Put warning signs on your property, keep him out of threatening situations, and muzzle him when you take him out. If anyone asks, tell him, "Yes, he does bite. Please leave him alone."

Not long ago, a child in a New York suburb chased a ball through a neighbor's back yard and was attacked and killed by the neighbor's dog. Many dog owners, I'm sorry to say, are too quick to explain the tragedy away by citing the child's foolishness in running into a strange dog's yard. Foolishness is not a capital offense. The dog's owners were morally responsible.

Be honest with yourself about your dog's temperament. If he becomes dangerous, and you can't keep him out of situations where he's likely to bite, take him to the vet and have him put to sleep. Don't be sentimental about a dog who is a threat to your community. You can be sentimental about your next one.

Finally, I should say something about how to face an aggressive dog. This will undoubtedly be someone else's dog. Yours, with the expert care and socializing he'll get from you, will be the very soul of courtesy and good fellowship. However, we live in paranoid times, and a lot of irresponsible people are keeping vicious dogs. If you meet up with one, you should know what to do.

First of all, very few dogs bite without prior warning. Most of them would rather not bite you if they can scare you away. Before an aggressive attack, a dog will curl his lips up and forward exposing his canine teeth. He'll stare directly at you and snarl menacingly. His ears will be pricked forward (although he'll lay them back at the moment of attack), his hackles will be raised, and his legs and tail will be stiff. At this point he may still be warning you. If the display intensifies as you move forward, he's not kidding. If, on the other hand, he drops his tail and shifts his weight to his hind feet, he's probably bluffing. But don't press your luck. Every dog has his own personal territory. He may bluff you in the driveway and nail you on the front porch. Unless it's absolutely necessary to get past this dog, leave him alone, and don't advance on him.

All this seems pretty obvious. Nobody in his right mind is going to tangle with a snarling monster. But what are the alternatives? First of all, stand still, stand upright, and stare right back at him. Don't try to make friends, and for heaven's sake, *don't* squat down. At this point, you need every shred of dominance you can muster. If the owner is nearby, stand your ground and wait for him to come and collect his dog.

If you have to retreat, keep staring at him and back away slowly. *Never turn and run*. This will only trigger a prey-catching response and get you bitten from behind. As long as you maintain a dominant posture, the dog will probably approach to a certain distance and no farther. He may follow you, but every step he takes is a step in your favor. The farther he gets from his own territory, the less likely he is to attack you. If you have to back all the way to your car or your own front porch, do it.

The above situation is, I hope, an exaggeration. In a sane world, a dog this aggressive wouldn't be running around loose. However, if you're a door-to-door salesman, a mailman, or a Jehovah's Witness, you should know how to get yourself out of a protective dog's yard without losing a leg.

A purely aggressive dog is easy to recognize and not impossible to deal with if you keep your cool. The fear biter, on the other hand, is much more complicated. These dogs are probably responsible for more bites than the real meanies. The problem is that the fear biter puts out a mixed set of signals. He may show you a completely submissive (i.e., friendly) facial expression—ears back, eyes averted—and at the same time raise his hackles and stiffen his legs and tail. Don't mistake a stiff, nervously twitching tail for a friendly wag. If you reach down to pat him, or turn your back on him—bingo. He's just added you to his list of victims.

So follow the handler's motto and *read the whole dog*. Unless every sign is submissive and positive—face, tail, and body—leave him alone, and don't turn your back on him. As a general rule, ignore any dog who doesn't drive up in a welcome wagon, introduce himself, and invite you home to dinner. There's no law that says you have to make friends with every dog you meet.

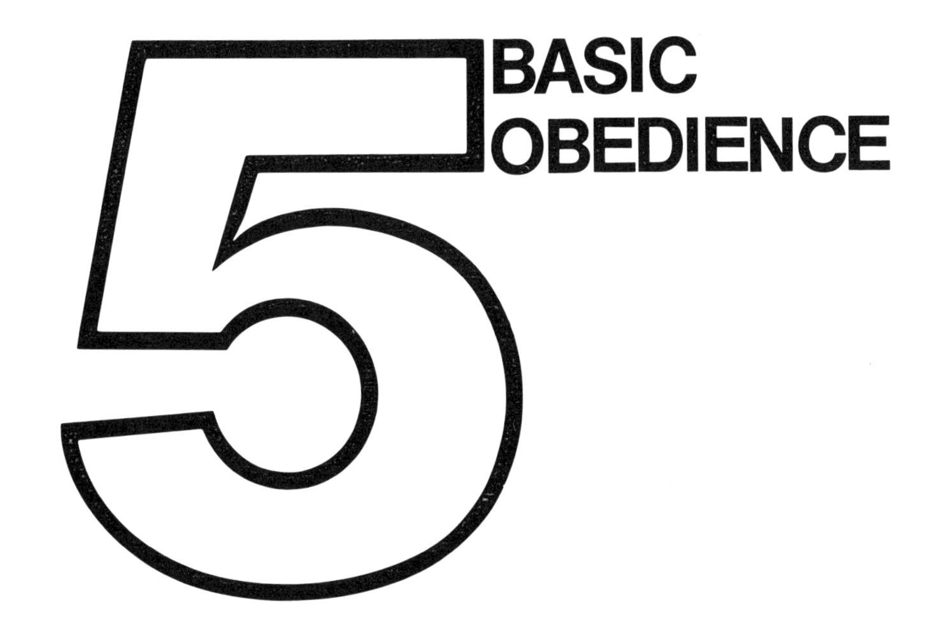

5 BASIC OBEDIENCE

Horsemen have an expression that I wish more dog owners knew. The word is *handy*. A handy horse is one that's even-tempered, sure-footed, and well-schooled; a horse you can ride anywhere. Your dog should be handy, too. He ought to be able to lie down and wait for you in a store while you go through agonies of indecision in the dressing room. He ought to be able to sit quietly in an elevator without cold-nosing everyone who gets in. He ought to be able to walk next to you from your car to your door even when his lead is at the bottom of your pocketbook under an armload of groceries. He ought to come when you call him, follow where you lead, and stay where you park him. This is the basic purpose of obedience training.

A lot of obedience enthusiasts are obsessed with the number of points their dogs collect in the show ring, forgetting that the fundamental goal of their training is to turn out a handy dog. It stands to reason that if your dog can go anywhere and do anything, you'll have more fun with him. And isn't that why you got him in the first place?

So let's begin at the beginning. You can start teaching your puppy to stand still and sit when he's about ten weeks old. You can also start at ten months, ten years, or any age that you think it's time he started learning to behave himself. He won't be a genius at ten weeks, but you'll be surprised at how much he can learn if you devote three to five minutes of daily play time to these two simple exercises.

The stand-stay is a required obedience exercise in the show ring. Even if you don't plan to show your dog, it doesn't hurt to have one who will stand still while you're bathing or grooming him. You'll get the job over with a lot faster if you have both hands free to work with.

Get down on the floor next to your dog. He should be standing or sitting with his head toward your right. Hook one or two fingers of your right hand around his collar, under his chin. Place the back of your left hand under his tummy just ahead of his hind legs. Now, gently pull forward with your right hand and lift up with your left. If he's been sitting, this should make him stand. If he's standing, just keep a light pressure against his collar and tummy. Hold it and give the command, "Stand . . . stay." Praise him in a soothing voice until he stands with no resistance. Take your hands away slowly, first the left, then the right. If he moves, sits, or lies down, don't say anything unkind. Give him a warning "No." Do you remember the radio announcer who used to say, "Uh, uh, uh, don't touch that dial. Stay tuned for . . ."? Use *that* tone of voice. He's still too young for harsh corrections. (If you don't remember the radio announcer, ask your mother.) Put him back into position with a gentle tug on his collar and a lift under his tummy. "Stand." Hold him for a moment or two while you praise him. "Stay." Now let go again. If he moves, put him back.

STAND-STAY Get down on the floor next to your dog. He should be standing or sitting with his head toward your right. Hook one or two fingers of your right hand around his collar, under his chin. Place the back of your left hand under his tummy just ahead of his hind legs. Now, gently pull forward with your right hand and lift up with your left.

Remember to praise him while he's standing still. Keep your voice gentle and calm. If you sound too excited, he'll only want to jump around and play with you. Never repeat the same exercise more than five times in any one session. Your puppy probably won't figure it out the first day, or even the second or third, but he will eventually. Until he does, end every lesson holding him in place with lots of praise.

Your puppy has a very short attention span and a very long memory. Five minutes of training every day for a week will teach him more than one hour once a week. If his early lessons are a drag, he'll be an unwilling pupil for the rest of his life, so keep it short, lively, and fun.

After you've practiced the stand-stay for a few days, you can start teaching your puppy to sit. He won't be standing perfectly yet, but he'll be used to the idea. Incidentally, many trainers suggest teaching the stand and sit at the same time, alternating one with the other. If your dog is old enough to absorb two lessons at once, go ahead and try it. If you're working with a young puppy, however, I think you'll be more successful if you introduce only one idea at a time.

Begin with him in a standing position facing toward your right. Hook two fingers of your right hand under his collar at the back of his neck. Place your left hand on his back just ahead of his tail. Now, run your left hand back over his tail and down his hind legs toward his hocks. Then, with the heel of your left hand, nudge his hind legs forward just above the hocks in a tucking gesture. At the same time, pull gently backward on his collar with your right hand. This combined pull and tuck will compel even the biggest, dumbest, most stubborn dog to sit. While you're doing all this, give the command "Sit." As soon as his bottom hits the floor, tell him "Stay." If he resists, hold him in position and give him lots of praise until he relaxes. Then take your hands away. If he pops up, repeat the whole thing.

After he sits for several seconds without being held, tell him, "Stand," and lift him into position if necessary. Tell him, "Stay," and take your hands away. If he moves, put him back. If he holds it, praise him. Then repeat the sit exercise. Repeat each of these no more than five times, and then go out and play.

You've probably seen or used an earlier method of teaching a dog to sit whereby the trainer pulls back or up on the collar and forces the dog into a sitting position by pushing down on his hindquarters. A dog who didn't feel like

SIT Begin with your dog in a standing position facing toward your right. Hook two fingers of your right hand under his collar at the back of his neck. Place your left hand on his back just ahead of his tail and run it down his hind legs toward his hocks. Then, with the heel of your left hand, nudge his hind legs forward just above the hocks in a tucking gesture. At the same time, pull gently back on his collar with your right hand.

sitting would either squirm out from under or brace himself until he was forced to the floor. The tucking-in method, even though it may mean getting down on your knees, is both gentler and more effective than the old one. Don't forget, however, to start the exercise with your hand on his back just ahead of his tail. Eventually, he'll learn to anticipate your command, and he'll sit as soon as you touch his back without having to be tucked.

In time, you'll be able to stop using your left hand altogether. Your puppy will respond to a verbal command and a slight pressure on the front or back of his collar. When he consistently remembers the sit and stand without being lifted or tucked, you can start teaching him to lie down.

Put your dog on-lead and have him sit by your left side facing front. Kneel down on your left knee or both knees. Reach over his shoulder with your left hand and pick up his left front leg. Gently shake his leg up and down. If his foot flops loosely, terrific; that means he's nice and relaxed. If he's tense, talk to him, pat him a few times, and try it again. As soon as his left foot is loose and relaxed, drop it, and pick up his right leg in your right hand. Shake it until he's relaxed. All this may sound a little silly, but I can promise you that a tense dog is not going to want to lie down for you. If you flip him or force him down, you'll only upset him more, and he'll bounce back up as soon as you take your hands off him. A lot of potential training problems can be prevented by introducing each new exercise in as pleasant and natural a way as possible. So take your time with this one. Don't try to make him lie down until he's relaxed and happy.

As soon as he's nice and loose, fold your lead up in your right hand until it's just long enough for you to reach his right elbow. Now, reach over his back with your left hand. With both hands, pick up both forelegs and cradle your dog against your body as if you were teaching him to sit up and beg. Don't worry if he chooses this moment to give you a big sloppy wet kiss. It only proves that he's having a good time. Gently twist his body clockwise and lower him to the ground on his right side. At the same time, give the command "Down." Say it like this: "Dooooowwwwwnnnnn."

Keep your left hand on his shoulder so he won't bounce up and tell him "Stay." Don't worry if he rolls over on his back. Rub his tummy and tell him how clever he is. Praise him in a calm, soothing voice and slowly take your hand away. Let him lie there for a few seconds and then release him.

If you can't lift your dog, you can get him to lie down by sliding his front feet forward until his elbows touch the floor. This method will not work well, however, if your dog is tense or resists lying down. Furthermore, it will be much easier for him to pop up from this position since he'll be lying with his hind feet under him. So, if you use this technique, be sure your dog is relaxed and in an agreeable mood before you try it.

When you release your dog at the end of an exercise, tell him "OK," and let him come to you for lots of praise.

DOWN Have your dog on lead and sit him by your left side facing front. Reach over his shoulder with your left hand and pick up his left front leg. Gently shake his leg up and down until he's relaxed. Pick up his right leg in your right hand and do the same thing. As soon as your dog is relaxed, fold your lead up in your right hand until it's just long enough for you to reach his right elbow. Now, reach over his back with your left hand. With both hands, pick up both forelegs and cradle your dog. Gently twist his body clockwise and lower him to the ground on his right side.

Keep practicing stands, sits, and downs on lead until he responds in each case to a verbal command and a light tug on his collar—back for sits, forward for stands, and downward for down.* Don't press all this on him too quickly, and don't get into the habit of yanking him into position with your lead. That tug on the collar is only a reminder. If he doesn't respond to it, get down on your knees and use both hands.

Some dogs resist lying down either because they are too nervous to lie still or too dominant to accept a submissive position. If your puppy has had lots of affectionate handling since the day you got him, he shouldn't object too strenuously. Don't rush him. If you have to spend a couple of days picking his feet up and putting them down again, do it. It'll pay off in the long run. Practice the other exercises first. Doing something he knows how to do, and being praised for it, will help put him in the right frame of mind. Try having him sit for a full minute or more before making him lie down. By that time he'll be a little tired of holding his front end up and should be more receptive.

Always end each training session with an exercise he does well—or less badly. If he hates to lie down but sits like an angel, end with a sit. Even when you get farther along in your training, go back to something he already knows to finish each session. Ending each day on a positive note will do a lot for his attitude and yours.

All of the above exercises can be practiced at home in the normal course of playing with your puppy. Don't expect instant results. As he gets older, he'll learn new things much more quickly. For the time being, practice each exercise every day no more than five times. None of these is physically taxing or requires a sustained attention span, so you can start them at an early age. If you're raising an eighty-pounder, your life will be a lot easier if you can teach him to sit and lie down when he weighs only twenty pounds. So get the jump on him.

When you get ready to start strict on-lead training (when your puppy is at least four months old), you'll have to invest in a new collar. For years, the standard training collar was a chain-link choker. Today, however, most good trainers recommend a braided or woven nylon choker with a metal ring at each end. It's lighter, quieter, easier on a dog's coat, stronger (believe it or not), and cheaper than a chain collar. Some pet shops haven't caught on to this yet, so you may have to shop around to find one. Take the trouble. It's worth it.

While I'm on the subject of collars, you'll probably see more than a few idiots walking around the streets with dogs wearing spiked chain chokers. These are designed to poke dull spikes into the dog's neck every time he pulls on his lead. Forget them. A properly handled dog doesn't need one, and an

* In thinking about getting your dog down without falling on your face, you probably forgot all about your lead. However, if you had it properly folded in your right hand, it gave the signal automatically when you twisted his body and laid him down or when you slid his front feet forward.

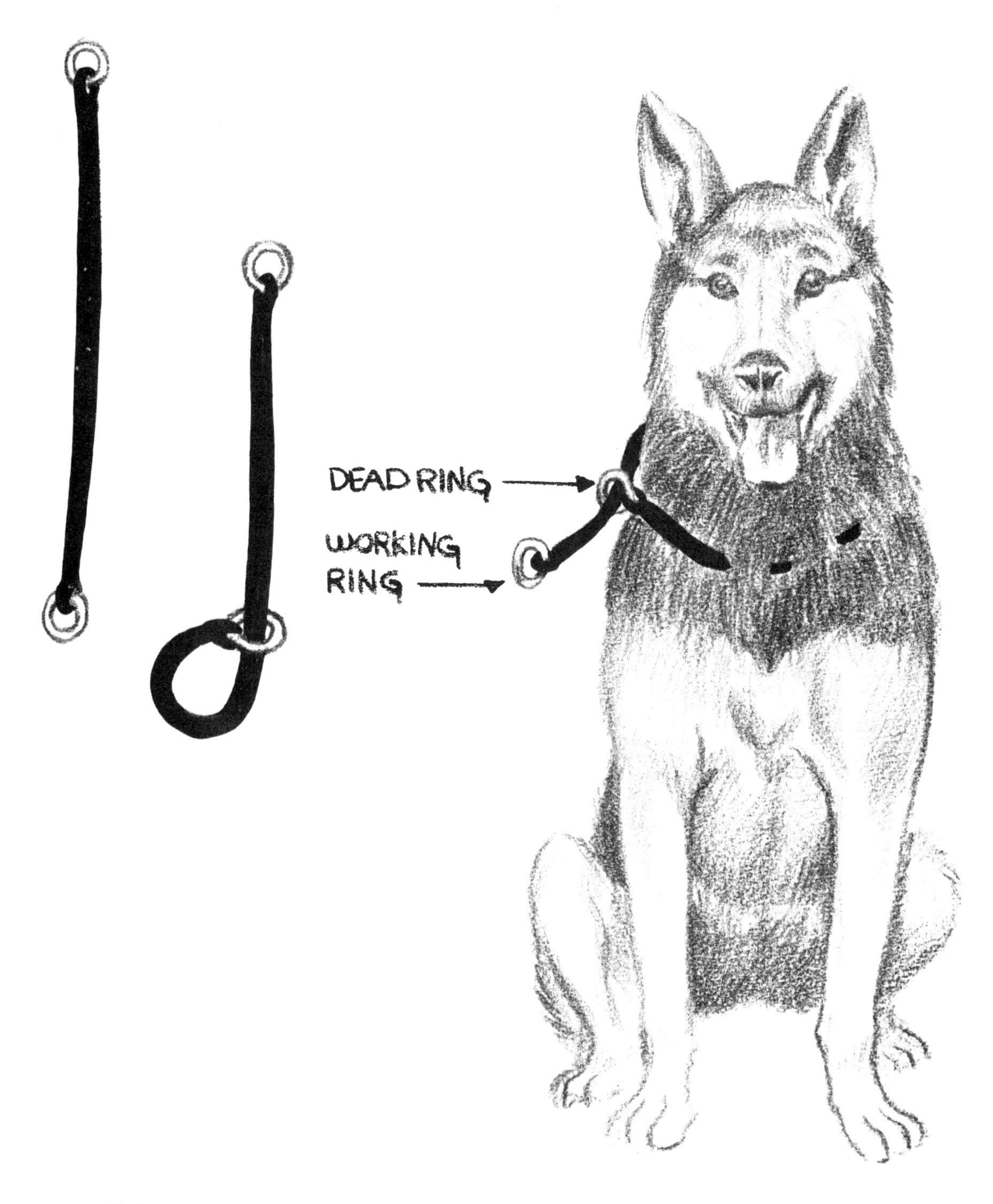

COLLAR Put your dog's collar on exactly as shown. If it's on any other way, it won't release properly.

improperly handled dog will get hurt by one. Whoever invented this device and made it available to unskilled dog owners ought to be made to wear one himself. If you're a bondage freak or think that your dog looks tougher—hence making you look tougher—with a chain around his neck, stick to smooth links or buy him a necklace. We normal folks will use nylon.

Take your dog with you when you go out to buy a collar. The right one should be big enough to slip over his head and ears without hurting him but should not extend more than three or four inches when pulled tight.

I'm not being picky about this. If your dog's collar is on backward, it won't release properly when he's walking by your left side in the heel position. If you can't jerk and release effectively, the collar won't work for you. So look at the illustration again and be sure you've got it right.

Your lead should be four to six feet long and made of cotton or nylon webbing, or very, very flexible leather. I like cotton the best. Nylon is too slippery, and leather is too stiff. No chains allowed. The clasp on your lead shouldn't be any bigger or heavier than necessary.

Once you get your dog decked out, think about your own clothing. Wear flat, nonskid shoes and straight-legged pants. No baggy bell-bottoms or flowing skirts, please. Your dog will be working close to you and won't enjoy it with yards of fabric flapping in his face.

Check your collar again to be sure it's on straight. Snap your lead on the dead ring, the one that does *not* tighten the collar when you pull it. In general, you'll be using this ring whenever you teach your dog a new exercise. This is to avoid giving him an unpleasant sensation at the very moment he's learning something new. Save the working ring for those times when you run into problems that need sharp correction. Don't worry, you'll have plenty of chances to use it, and it will be that much more effective if your dog hasn't grown accustomed to it.

Now, let's get the kid outdoors and see what he can do. Run through your stand, sit, and down exercises a couple of times to get him in the mood. Then, with your dog sitting by your left side, slip the loop of your lead over your right thumb and fold it into the palm of your hand until you can hold it waist high without too much slack. Place your left hand, palm down, over your lead and hold it comfortably at your side.

PREPARATION FOR HEEL With your dog sitting by your left side, slip the loop of your lead over your right thumb and fold it into the palm of your hand until you can hold it waist high without too much slack. Place your left hand, palm down, over your lead and hold it comfortably at your side.

Ready, set, go. "Puppy, heeeel!" Sound enthusiastic. Start off with your left foot, and give the command as you take your first step. If he isn't dead on his feet, he'll probably start right up with you. If he doesn't, don't yank. How's he supposed to know what "Heel!" means? Pat him on the head with your left hand, and then swing your left hand out in front of him so he follows it. Encourage him. "Come on, puppy. Let's go."

Once you get him moving, keep him next to you. If he drifts off to the left, give him a tug to the right with your left hand down at collar level. If he's little, you'll have to bend over. Keep moving, and give him lots of praise as soon as he gets back in line.

If you have an eager fellow who forges ahead of you, give him a backward tug every time he starts to move ahead. Don't stop, though. I know it's a little hard to tug backward and move forward at the same time, but you'll get it. Keep moving, and keep praising him whenever he's in position. His shoulder should be just about in line with your hip, but don't worry about perfection yet. At this point, you just want to keep him moving close to your left side without lagging or forging too much.

If you have a large, ambitious dog on whom a few tugs with the dead ring seem to have no effect, switch to the working ring. Settle the collar high on his neck just under his chin where you'll have more leverage. Then give him a sharp jerk and release every time he starts to pull away. Use two hands if you have to. If he's a big strong fellow, don't be afraid to give him a few very hard jerks. A couple of really stiff corrections will do a lot more good than a lot of wishy-washy ones. Don't forget to praise him as soon as he responds. As soon as he gets the message, put him back on the dead ring.

OK. Now, you've gone a dozen paces or so, and your dog is paddling along next to you wondering what's up. Lay on an about-turn. Don't do a military reverse; it looks nice on the parade ground, but it's too quick for a dog. Make your turn with three pivot steps to the right, and keep your feet moving. Call your dog's name as you make your turn and guide him around with your left hand at collar level. (You've probably guessed by now why I like big dogs. I hate all that bending over.)

Half the secret to good heeling is attention. Keep up a steady stream of chitchat so he doesn't get bored. Use his name every time his attention wanders.

After you've done a couple of about-turns, try a halt. Now pay attention. This will sound a little like rubbing your stomach, patting your head, and twirling hoops around your ankles all at the same time, but hang in there.

First, your feet. Begin your halt with your right foot in front of you. Bring your left foot up next to it and stop. This isn't nit-picking. Your left leg is the one

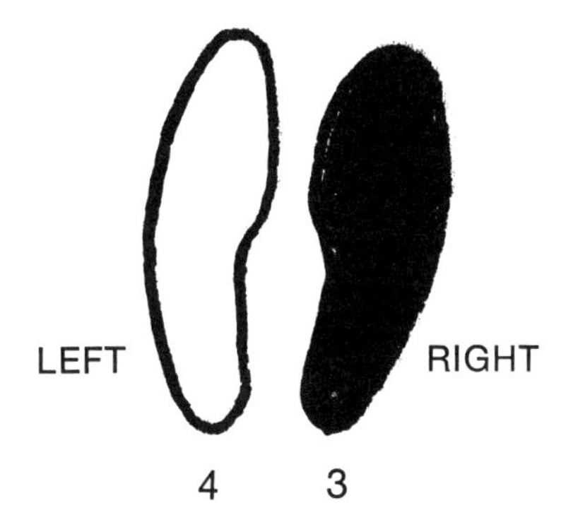

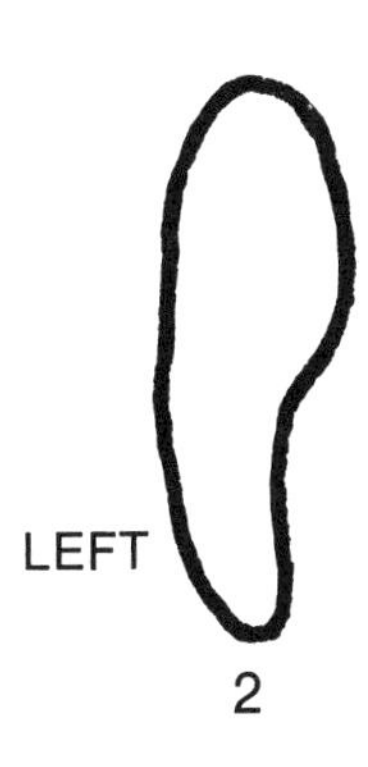

HALT As you're walking, right, left, right, left, begin the halt with your right foot in front of you. Bring your left foot up next to it and stop. Your left leg is the one closest to your dog, and it's the one he follows. It should be the first one to move when you start out and the last one to stop moving when you halt.

closest to your dog, and it's the one he follows. Therefore it should be the first one to move when you start out and the last one to stop moving when you halt.

This is what you do with your hands while you're trying to remember your feet: Bring your right hand around and take hold of your lead about four or five inches above the clasp. Tug back gently. At the same time, let go of the lead with your left hand and place it on your dog's back just ahead of his tail. "Puppy, sit." If he doesn't respond right away, slide your left hand down over his rear and tuck him into a sit.

It helps if you have rhythm. When your right foot is in front of you, call the dog's name. Then, as you bring your left foot up to meet your right, transfer your hands and say "Sit. Goooood boy."

Now, start all over again. Heel him back and forth a couple of times, remembering to call his name and get your left hand down to collar level whenever you turn. Then halt. If you haven't tripped over your own feet yet, you can start practicing left and right turns. These, too, require a little fancy footwork. Alway pivot on your inside foot, left for left turns, right for right turns. If you don't, you'll either step away from your dog before he notices, or you'll walk into him. Both tend to discourage close heeling.

Repeat the sits, stands, and downs a couple of times before calling it a day. Remember, always finish a training session with an exercise your dog knows well. Then tell him he's the best dog in the whole world and take him out for ice cream.

That's about it. Practice heeling for fifteen minutes or so every day. Whatever problems you run into will probably result from lack of attention or sloppy footwork. So don't forget those dance-step diagrams. Remember, your dog's head is down there by your knees, if not your ankles, and he's going to be watching your feet. Precise footwork will make every lesson that much clearer.

You say you're a ninety-pound weakling with a hundred-and-twenty-pound monster, and you feel as if he's towing you down the street on water

SIT Bring your right hand around and take hold of the lead about four or five inches above the clasp. Tug back gently. At the same time, let go of the lead with your left hand and place it on your dog's back just ahead of his tail. Command: "Sit."

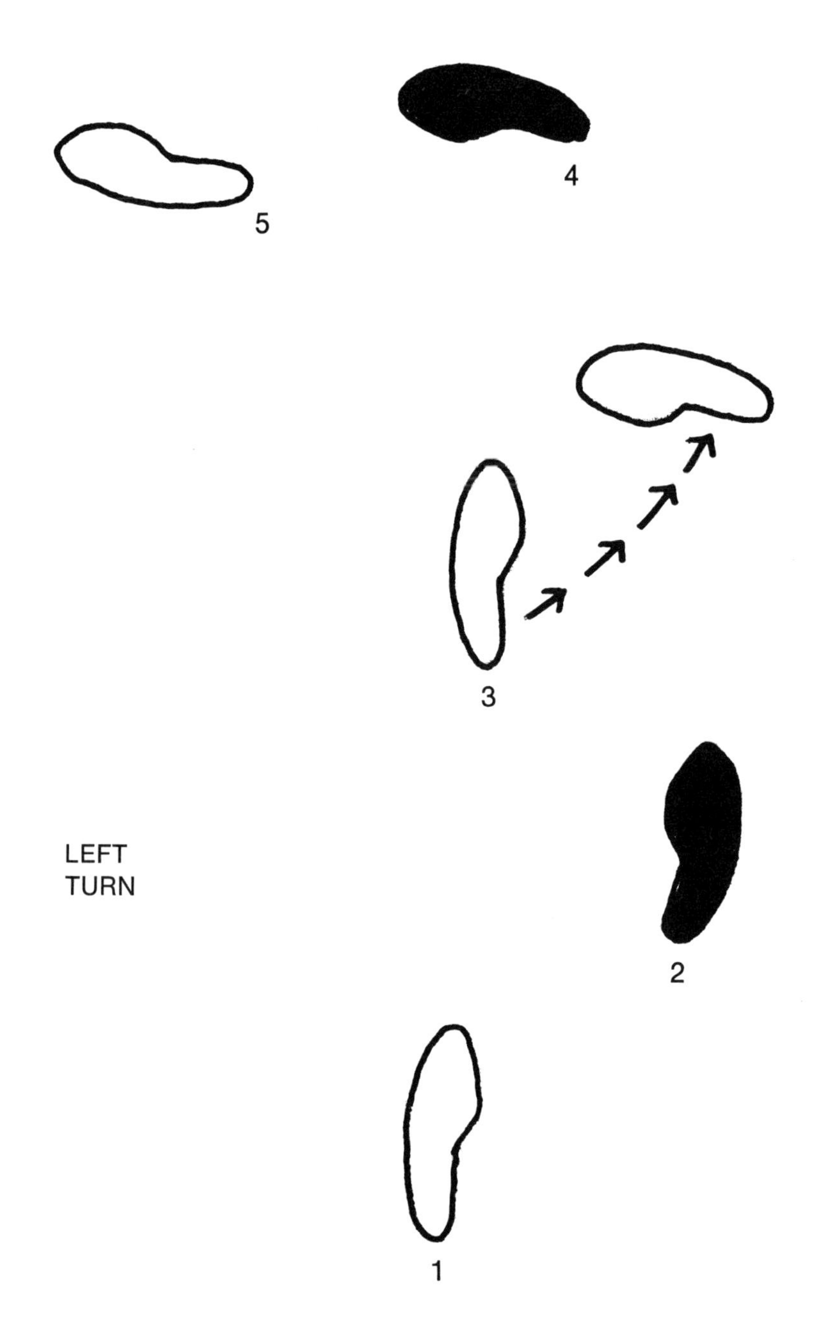

LEFT TURN—RIGHT TURN Follow the diagram carefully for your footwork. And remember—always pivot on your inside foot, left for left turns, right for right turns.

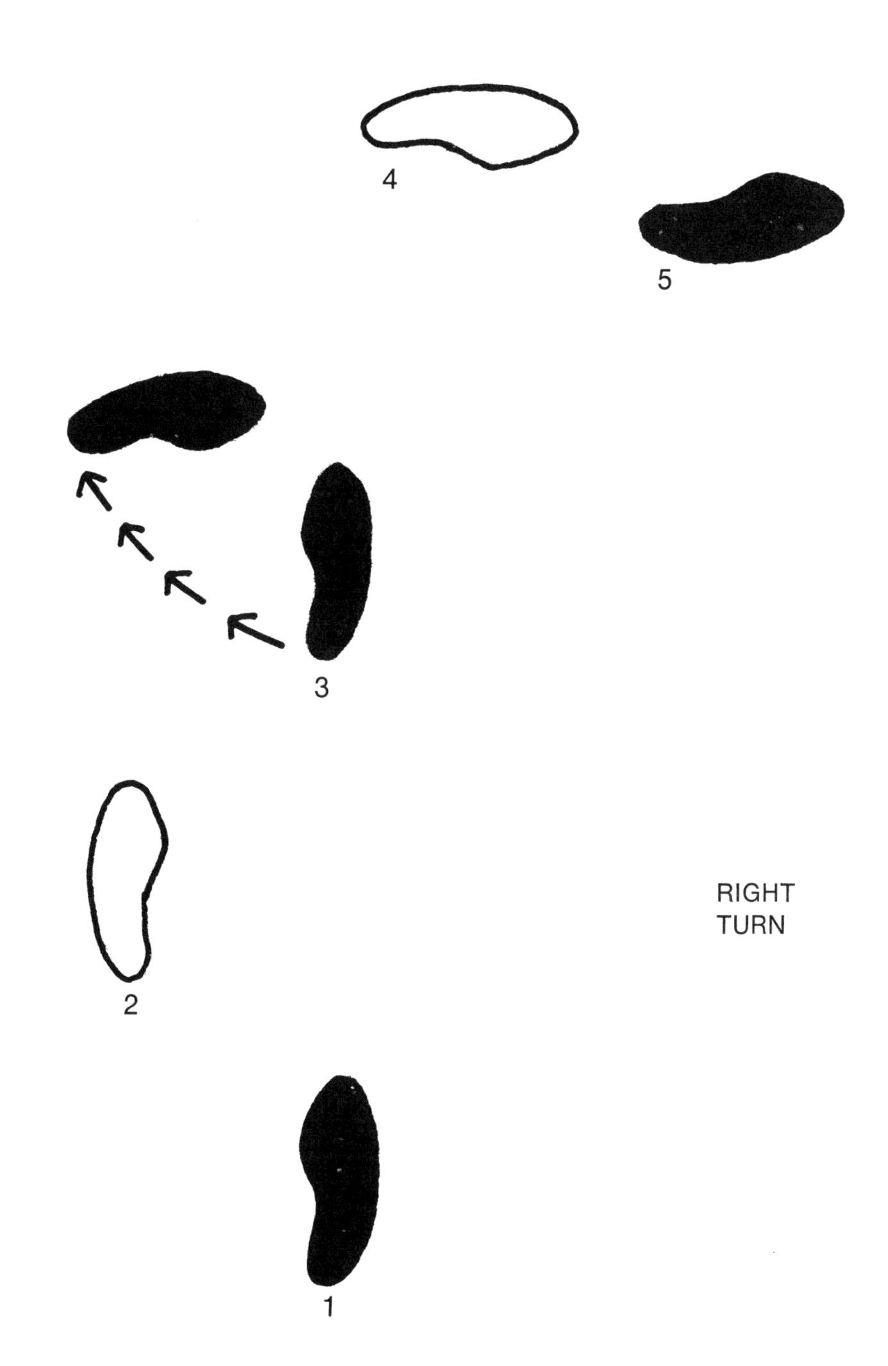

RIGHT
TURN

skis? Try this. Snap your lead on the working ring and pass the lead around behind your body. Fold it up into your right hand so that you have only a couple of inches of slack. Plant your right hand on your right hip. Now, when he tries to take off with you, you'll have all your body weight to correct with rather than just the strength of your arms. Just as he starts to pull ahead, stop quickly, and tell him to sit. Praise him as soon as he responds. Then start up again. When he shapes up, put him back on the dead ring and hold your lead normally.

If your dog starts lagging behind you, encourage him with your voice and a pat. Don't get into the habit of jerking your lead to make him keep up. If he has the slightest spark of independence, jerking will only make him lag more. If he forges ahead, don't let him drag you. And don't try to drag him. Put your lead on the working ring, and give him a few corrective jerks. Be sure to give him some slack after each jerk and praise him as long as he stays in position. Go back to the dead ring as soon as he stops forging.

Keep it lively. Don't walk more than fifteen paces without stopping or changing direction. (Incidentally, another good forging correction is to turn around and go the other way as soon as he gets ahead of you; this will teach him to pay attention.) Keep your walk brisk and businesslike. If you have a tiny dog who can't keep up, shorten your steps. This will slow your forward speed without your pace getting sluggish. Also, try to walk with your heels close to the ground—as if you were wearing scuffs—if you're training a toy breed or a dachschund. This will help keep him from shying away from your feet.

Vary your pace from time to time. Jog a few steps. Take a few slow-motion steps. Do this whenever his attention wanders. Don't rely on your lead to hold his attention. Talk to him. If he seems bored, entertain him. Walk on tiptoe for a few paces. Try goose-stepping. Do your Charlie Chaplin imitation. He'll think you're so crazy, he won't take his eyes off you.

Don't be in a mad rush to start him heeling off-lead. Most obedience schools put their beginners through a ten-week course before even thinking about it. So take it easy. When you get around to it, he'll be that much more reliable. When he starts heeling well without a constant stream of reminders and corrections, you can start working with your left hand off the lead. Don't get lazy, though. If he needs a correction, use your left hand. Before you take your lead off, practice with it hanging over your right shoulder where you can grab it in a hurry. If all goes well, you can start removing it for a couple of minutes during each practice session. If you need to make corrections, put it back on.

Your voice and body will be your only means of holding your dog's attention when you start working off-lead. Keep talking. Call his name every time you make a turn. Vary your pace and direction. Don't follow him. Make him follow you. You can even make a game out of this. By now he should understand what heeling is even if he's a little sloppy. He should know that he must stick by your left side, turn when you turn, and stop when you stop. So try to run away from him. When he catches up, turn quickly and run the other way. Dodge to the side. Stop quickly and start again. He'll love it.

I realize that in normal walks you won't be darting around and talking to your dog every second. Furthermore, in the show ring, you're not allowed to give more than a single command at the beginning of each exercise. Actually, the single hardest heeling exercise of all would be to walk half a mile in a straight line without speaking to your dog. A lot of prize-winning obedience dogs probably couldn't do it. To get this far, your dog will have to be a confirmed, habitual heeler. The only way to build that habit is by the methods I've described.

The sit- and down-stays are two of the easiest and most useful obedience exercises you can teach your dog. Once he learns them, you'll find yourself using them constantly.

Begin with your dog sitting by your left side in the heel position. Put his lead on the dead ring and hold it folded in your right hand with your left hand free. Swing your left hand out and back toward your dog's face with the palm flat. Don't bump him in the nose. At the same time, give the command "Stay" and step away from him with your right foot. (If you start with your left foot, he'll want to go with you.) Walk out to the end of the lead, turn, and face him.

If he tries to go with you, tell him "No" and put him back in a sit. Repeat the "Stay" signal, and leave him again. While you're standing out there at the end of your lead, hold it in your left hand. Don't stare at your dog. Look at a spot about a foot over his head. If he starts to break, step forward on your right foot and swing upward with your right hand, catching the lead and lifting it up. Tell him "Sit!" As soon as he sits, drop the lead from your right hand, hold your hand at about waist level, palm toward your dog, and tell him "Stay."

Don't talk to your dog while he's in a sit- or down-stay. You'll only encourage him to break. Slowly walk back toward him, around behind him, and come up to a halt on his right side. Then lay on the praise.

Gradually increase your time at the end of the lead until he will sit-stay for

SIT-STAY Begin with your dog sitting by your left side in the heel position. Put his lead on the dead ring and hold it folded in your right hand with your left hand free. Swing your left hand out and back toward your dog's face with the palm flat. At the same time, give the command "Stay" and step away

from him with your right foot. Walk out to the end of the lead, turn and face him with the lead in your left hand. Look at a spot about a foot above your dog's head. If he starts to break, step forward on your right foot and swing upward with your right hand, catching the lead and lifting it up. Say "Sit."

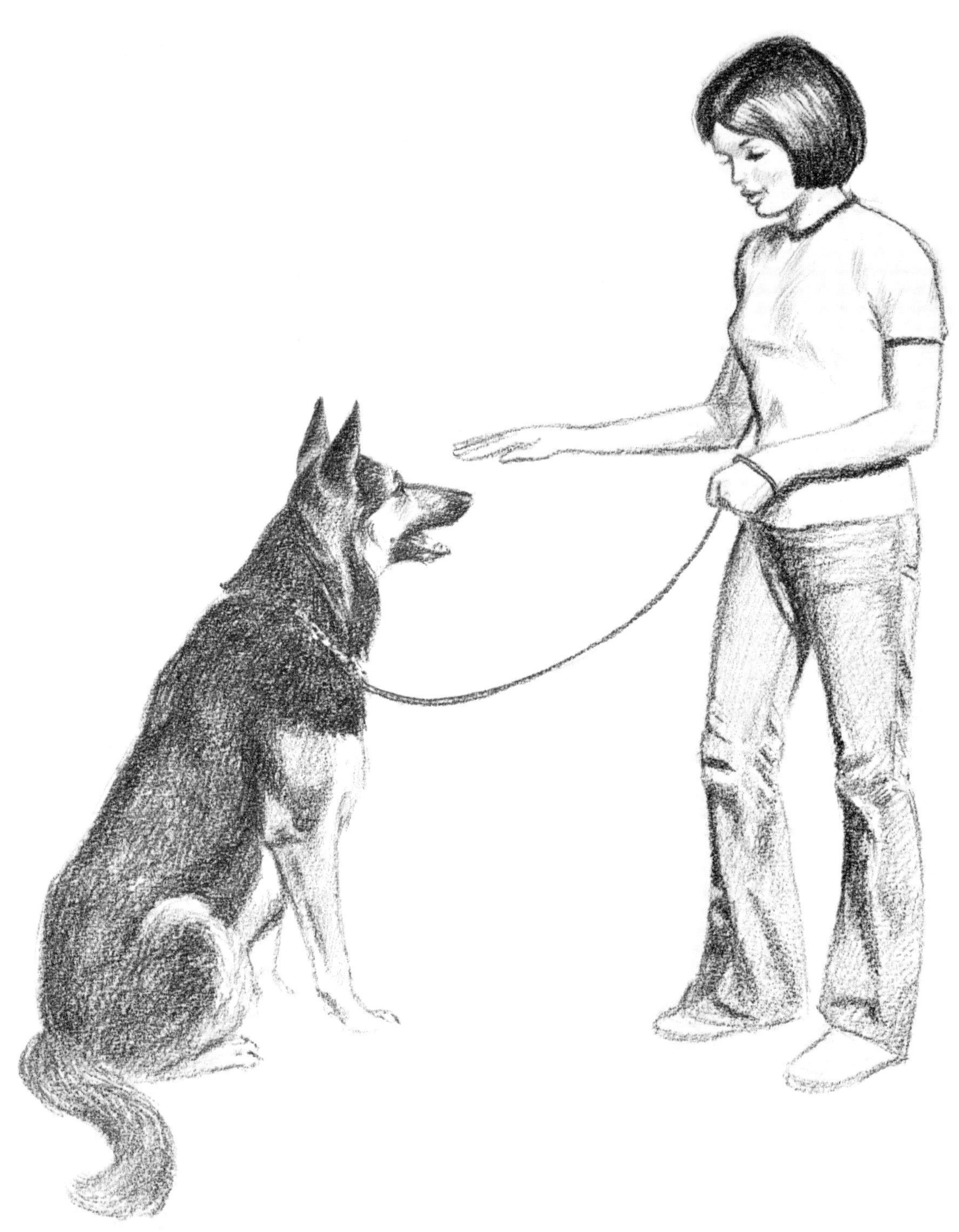

SIT-STAY As soon as your dog sits, drop the lead from your right hand, hold your hand at about waist level, palm toward your dog, and say "Stay."

about a minute and a half. Then try this. Tell him to sit-stay and walk out to the end of the lead. Drop the lead on the ground in front of you. Return to your dog. Pause a moment. Then tell him to stay again and walk away about fifteen feet or so before turning to face him. If he breaks, practice a couple of on-lead sit-stays before trying it again. As soon as he's got this one figured out, you can practice your sit-stays off-lead.

If you decide to show your dog, he will have to hold a sit-stay for a full minute while you stand across the ring from him. If you get into open classes, he'll have to hold it for three minutes while you leave the ring and go out of sight. However, in normal everyday life, if you want your dog to stay in one spot for more than a couple of minutes, tell him to lie down. He'll be more comfortable and less likely to move.

To teach the down-stay, begin with your dog sitting on your left in the heel position. Hold your lead in your right hand. With the same hand, reach down as if to pat the ground in front of your dog. As you do so, hit the lead with your left hand creating a downward tug on his collar. Tell him "Down!"

By now, he should respond to a verbal command and a downward tug. If he doesn't, lay him down by lifting his front legs and turning his body. Once he's down, give him the "Stay" command (palm toward his face) and step out to the end of the lead. (Did you remember to leave on your right foot?)

If he breaks after you leave him, go back, lay him down, and leave him again. Some trainers suggest stepping on your lead to give a downward tug rather than going back to your dog. This may work for you if you have long legs or a large dog. However, you need a sharp downward angle from your dog's collar to your foot in order to give a clear signal. If stepping on your lead jerks him forward, you'll only confuse him. If you're not sure of the angle, or it doesn't work the first time you try it, forget it. Go back and lay him down from the heel position. He'll learn much faster if you take the trouble to give him clear signals. So don't be lazy.

Once he gets to the point where you can step out to the end of the lead for a couple of minutes without his moving, you can start dropping your lead and crossing the room just as you did with the sit-stay. Once he masters this, you can try walking around the room a couple of times while he stays. You'll want to get him used to seeing you move around without following. Then you

DOWN-STAY Begin with your dog sitting on your left in the heel position. Hold your lead in your right hand. With the same hand, reach down as if to pat the ground in front of the dog, and as you do so, hit the lead with your left

hand, creating a downward tug on his collar. Say "Down." Once he's down, give him the "Stay" command (palm toward his face) and step out to the end of the lead. If he starts getting up, try to correct him by stepping on his lead.

can begin leaving the room for short periods of time. When you first try this, be sure you have some means of spying on him while you're out of sight. Peek through a crack in the door or find a spot where you can watch him in a mirror. If he breaks, go back and put him down again. Then leave him and stay in sight for a minute or so. Heel him around a few times for variety's sake. Then put him in a down-stay and go out of sight again. Return to him before he breaks (even if you're only away a few seconds) and give him lots and lots of praise.

Don't do all your practicing at home. Once he's working well in your own yard or apartment, take him out to a shopping center or a park and make him stay while people, dogs, and bikes go by. If he's going to be trustworthy, he's got to learn to tolerate distractions.

Having a dog who will stay where you park him can make your life as a dog owner a lot easier. You can tell him to wait in another room while you answer the door; you can leave him with the luggage while you consult the ticket agent; and best of all, you don't have to take him into the cubicle with you when you visit a public rest room.

If you leave your dog in a strange place, he's bound to be a little uneasy. If you must go out of sight, leave something of yours with him for reassurance—a jacket, an umbrella, even your pocketbook. The chances of someone stealing it with your dog lying on it are pretty slim. (But take your wallet anyway.) Don't, however, go out of sight if your pet is friendly enough to go away with a nice dog thief.

If you want your dog to stay put in a store or at a friend's house, have him lie down under a table, in a corner, or against a wall. He'll feel more secure and will be less likely to go exploring.

Practice the sit- and down-stays every day. Once he's doing them off-lead, you won't have to make special time for them. Tell him to stay in the bedroom while you brush your teeth. Have him stay in the corner while you fix his dinner. Practice whenever you think of it, but don't repeat any one exercise more than five times in a row. This is especially true of the stay exercises. Dogs find them very boring.

One of dog owners' most common and frustrating complaints is "He won't come when I call him." Having spent several of my formative years chasing a wirehaired fox terrier who darted off whenever I got within six feet of him, I can certainly sympathize. So let me tell you what I've learned since then.

First of all, don't chase him. He'll only think it's a terrific game. Call him and turn right around and run away from him. Ninety-nine times out of a hundred, he'll chase you. When he catches you, praise him to the skies. No matter how long it has taken you to get him, don't punish him when he finally comes. Grit your teeth and tell him how wonderful he is.

If you've made a practice of praising your puppy every time he comes to you, you shouldn't have a serious problem. However, there are a few independent souls who insist on going their own way no matter what. If your dog is one of these, you're going to have to inculcate an automatic, habitual response to the word "Come," and it won't happen overnight.

Put your dog in a sit-stay and step out to the end of the lead. Stand facing him for a few moments and then call, "Puppy, come!" Give a gentle tug on your lead at the same time. Be sure to keep your hands at collar level so that you're clearly pulling toward you and not upward. Fold your lead up as he approaches so he doesn't trip over it. When he reaches you, lift up on your lead and tell him "Sit." Don't drag him in to you with your lead. That tug is only a signal. If he doesn't respond, reach out with your hands as if you were going to pat him or feed him. Clap your hands and call him again. In this exercise especially, you must rely on your voice and hands more than your lead. After all, the whole point of it is to teach him to come when he's off-lead.

As soon as he consistently responds to your command without a tug on the lead or any other encouragement, try it off-lead. If you can find a narrow hall or alleyway to practice this in the first few times, so much the better.

The second *come* exercise is often called a *come-fore* in training classes. It's not a required obedience exercise, but it's very helpful in teaching your dog to come when he's running away from you, which is exactly when you need his obedience the most.

Start walking forward with your dog heeling next to you. Stop quickly and shuffle backward a few steps. Your dog will keep going forward. Let your lead unfold and play out. When your dog is almost out to the end of the lead, call him: "Puppy, come!" As he comes, fold your lead up quickly to get it out of the way, but keep your hands low. When he reaches you, lift your hands and tell him "Sit." Praise him lavishly.

Getting your dog to come in an obedience class or training session and getting him to come when he's taking off after a squirrel are two different matters. The second will take a lot longer to achieve, but this is the only way he'll learn it. Practice it every single day.

Lots of people will tell you to take a couple of dog biscuits with you whenever you take your dog out for a run. That way you'll be able to bribe him into coming back to you when you want to go home. This is a bad habit to get into. The dumbest dog in the world knows when you have food on you and when you don't. The day will come when you'll have no bribe handy and your dog will be taking off across a six-lane highway. So don't fall for shortcuts. The only sure way is the hard way: practice, practice, practice until your dog's response to the word "come" is habitual and automatic.

The finish is the final flourish to every obedience exercise—the icing on the cake. Dogs love it, probably because it's the last thing they do before they get praised, and it will impress the daylights out of any onlooker. The finish goes like this: Your dog comes and sits in front of you. After a second, you tell him "Puppy, heel!" He either nips around behind you or swivels around to the left and ends up sitting next to you in heel position. Usually with a smug look on his face.

Your dog can finish in either direction just as long as he ends up sitting by your left side. Every dog seems to be born with a preference for one direction or the other. So if you start teaching him one way and he hates it, try the other.

This is the first way: With your dog sitting in front of you, reach down with your left hand and take hold of his lead about four inches from the clasp. With your left foot, take a step backward and to your left—toward about 7:30 on an imaginary clock. Give the command "Puppy, heel" and guide him around counterclockwise with your left hand. When he gets almost all the way around, bring your left foot back up next to your right. This will bring him up next to you. When he gets there, tell him to sit. Be sure to make a wide sweep with your left hand so he has plenty of room to get his rear end around before you step forward. Keep practicing this until he learns to pivot around by himself without your stepping back and guiding him. If you have a show-off on your hands, don't be surprised if he leaps up, twists himself around in midair, and lands in heel position. Poodles are notorious for this. If you've got it, flaunt it.

If you plan to show your dog, I would advise using this finish as long as your dog doesn't actually loathe it. The reason is that if your dog finishes in a crooked position (you lose a couple of points for every crooked sit), he can straighten himself out with a continuation of the same motion. This makes corrections less confusing for him. If he goes around behind you and overshoots his mark, he's going to want to keep going in circles until he gets it right.

The second method of finishing is often easier for big dogs. Begin with your dog sitting in front of you. Fold your lead up in your right hand until you can hold it down in front of you with almost no slack. Give the command "Puppy, heel." Take a half-step backward with your right foot and start guiding him around clockwise with your right hand. As soon as he starts moving, take a whole step backward with your left foot—so that your left foot is farther back than your right. When your dog is behind you, transfer your lead from your right to left hand. Then bring your left foot up to meet your right. As soon as he's next to you, tell him to sit. Praise, praise, praise. When he figures this out, you can eliminate the footwork.

These are the basic obedience exercises. If you enter your dog in a novice obedience class at a dog show (sadly enough, only registered purebreds are eligible), he'll have to heel on- and off-lead, heel in a figure-eight on-lead, stand-stay while he's being examined by a judge (have a friend help you practice for this one), sit-stay off-lead for one minute, down-stay off-lead for three minutes, and come and finish off-lead. Just about any dog can be trained to do all this, and those who can make delightful pets.

Even if you have no intention of showing your dog, I think you'll find obedience training both useful and fun. And I never met a dog who didn't enjoy it. They definitely love the attention, and I suspect that they take a lot of satisfaction in knowing how to do things. Knowing how to behave, if he's been gently trained, can give confidence to a shy dog. If you have a rambunctious one, the rapport you establish in training can help you maintain control over him without a constant round of battles.

Although obedience training may not deal directly with whatever other problems you may have with your dog, these problems often solve themselves when you get into it. I'm not sure exactly why. It may simply be the extra attention and exercise. It may result from a change in attitudes or the owner's greater understanding of his dog. All I know is that it happens too often to be ignored.

Finally, a word about obedience schools. I've done the best I can to tell you how to teach the basic exercises to your dog. However, no book can ever be a complete substitute for live instruction. A professional trainer can spot your mistakes and tell you how to correct them in a few minutes. He can adapt general principles to your individual needs. The only thing he can't do—and shouldn't claim to do—is train your dog for you. There is little point in shelling out hundreds of dollars to have your dog trained to work for someone else. Once he comes home and discovers that you can't handle him, you're right back where you started—only poorer.

If you want professional help, look for a trainer who will teach you to train your own dog. Throughout the country, there are many nonprofit obedience-training clubs that hold classes for dog owners. They usually offer a ten-lesson course for around thirty dollars, and many of them welcome mongrels as well as purebreds. You go once a week, with your dog, and get instruction from a

LEFT FINISH With your dog sitting in front of you, reach down and take hold of the lead about four inches from the clasp. With your left foot, take a step backward and to your left. Command "Puppy, heel" and guide him around counterclockwise with your left hand. When he gets almost all the way around, bring your left foot back up next to your right. This will bring him up next to you. When he gets there, tell him to sit.

RIGHT FINISH Begin with your dog sitting in front of you. Fold your lead up in your right hand until you can hold it down in front of you with almost no slack. Give the command "Heel." Take a half step backward with your right foot and start guiding him around clockwise with your right hand. As soon as he starts moving, take a whole step backward with your left foot so that your left foot is farther back than your right. When your dog is behind you, transfer your lead from your right to left hand. Then bring your left foot up to meet your right. As soon as he's next to you, tell him to sit.

professional trainer. If you should decide to show your dog, the poise and experience he'll gain from working in a class with other dogs will be a great help. Obedience club courses are one of the last real bargains left in the dog world, and I recommend them highly. If you write to the American Kennel Club, they'll tell you how to get in touch with an obedience club in your area. Try it. It's fun.